# JEFFERSON
# DAVIS

Other titles in *Historical American Biographies*

**Annie Oakley**
*Legendary Sharpshooter*
ISBN 0-7660-1012-0

**John Wesley Powell**
*Explorer of the Grand Canyon*
ISBN 0-89490-783-2

**Benjamin Franklin**
*Founding Father and Inventor*
ISBN 0-89490-784-0

**Lewis and Clark**
*Explorers of the Northwest*
ISBN 0-7660-1016-3

**Buffalo Bill Cody**
*Western Legend*
ISBN 0-7660-1015-5

**Martha Washington**
*First Lady*
ISBN 0-7660-1017-1

**Clara Barton**
*Civil War Nurse*
ISBN 0-89490-778-6

**Paul Revere**
*Rider for the Revolution*
ISBN 0-89490-779-4

**Jeb Stuart**
*Confederate Cavalry General*
ISBN 0-7660-1013-9

**Robert E. Lee**
*Southern Hero of the Civil War*
ISBN 0-89490-782-4

**Jefferson Davis**
*President of the Confederacy*
ISBN 0-7660-1064-3

**Stonewall Jackson**
*Confederate General*
ISBN 0-89490-781-6

**Jesse James**
*Legendary Outlaw*
ISBN 0-7660-1055-4

**Susan B. Anthony**
*Voice for Women's Voting Rights*
ISBN 0-89490-780-8

**Thomas Alva Edison**
*Inventor*
ISBN 0-7660-1014-7

Historical American Biographies

# JEFFERSON DAVIS

## President of the Confederacy

Joann J. Burch

**Enslow Publishers, Inc.**

| 40 Industrial Road | PO Box 38 |
| Box 398 | Aldershot |
| Berkeley Heights, NJ 07922 | Hants GU12 6BP |
| USA | UK |

http://www.enslow.com

**Library of Congress Cataloging-in-Publication Data**

Burch, Joann Johansen.
    Jefferson Davis : president of the Confederacy / Joann J. Burch.
       p.  cm. — (Historical American biographies)
    Includes bibliographical references and index.
    Summary: Traces the life of the president of the Confederacy from his childhood, through his rise in Southern politics, and to his role as leader of the South during the Civil War.
    ISBN 0-7660-1064-3
    1. Davis, Jefferson, 1808–1889—Juvenile literature. 2. Statesmen—United States—Biography—Juvenile literature. 3. Presidents—Confederate States of America—Biography—Juvenile literature.
[1. Davis, Jefferson, 1808–1889. 2. Presidents—Confederate States of America.] I. Title. II. Series.
E467.1.D26B87 1998
973.7'13'092
[B]—DC21
                                   97-18046
                                      CIP
                                      AC

Printed in the United States of America

10 9 8 7 6 5 4

**To Our Readers:** We have done our best to make sure all Internet addresses in this book were active and appropriate when we went to press. However, the author and the publisher have no control over and assume no liability for the material available on those Internet sites or on other Web sites they may link to. Any comments or suggestions can be sent by e-mail to comments@enslow.com or to the address on the back cover.

**Illustration Credits:** Courtesy of "Beauvoir, the Jefferson Davis Shrine," pp. 42, 49, 100, 109; Enslow Publishers, Inc., pp. 46, 67; Library of Congress, pp. 6, 10, 15, 37, 75, 82, 95, 98, 103, 105, 110; Massachusetts Commandary Military Order of the Loyal Legion and the U.S. Army Military History Institute, pp. 8, 90; National Archives, pp. 68, 80, 85, 87, 96; National Archives, Sketch by James E. Kelly, p. 97; Photo by Joann J. Burch, pp. 17, 116.

**Cover Illustration:** Photo by Gene Boaz (Background); Library of Congress, Mathew Brady Collection (Inset).

# CONTENTS

*Jefferson Finis Davis*

| 1 |
|:-:|

# INAUGURATION

J efferson Davis spent the dreary morning of February 22, 1862, preparing for his inauguration as president of the Confederate States of America. Soon he would be standing beneath George Washington's statue on Capitol Square in Richmond, Virginia, to take the oath of office. He wanted to be the high-caliber leader that Washington had been, and Davis, a religious man, prayed "for the divine support I need so sorely."[1]

At noon Davis and Vice President Alexander Stephens were escorted to the hall of the House of Delegates. From there they led a grand procession from the Capitol to the public square. In spite of the cold winter rain, a crowd had gathered. An awning had been erected to protect Davis and the other dignitaries from the downpour.

Davis's wife, Varina, was driven to Capitol Square in a horse-drawn carriage. Walking on either side were four black footmen in black suits and white gloves. It seemed to Varina that they were on a funeral march, and she told the driver that the "pall-bearers" must leave. The driver was unhappy. "This, madam, is the way we always does in Richmond at funerals and sich-like," he explained.[2]

*Jefferson Davis was inaugurated for a six-year term as president of the Confederacy in Richmond, Virginia, on February 22, 1862, beneath the statue of George Washington in Capitol Square.*

At Capitol Square, Varina proudly watched her husband deliver his inaugural address. Tall and slender with neatly trimmed gray hair and beard, his boots blacked and polished, his suit immaculate, he gave dignity to the office of president.

"Fellow Citizens," Davis began,

> On this the birthday of the man most identified with the establishment of American independence, and beneath the monument erected to commemorate his heroic virtues and those of his compatriots, we have assembled to usher into existence the Permanent Government of the Confederate States.[3]

Davis described how the Confederate government hoped to preserve the ideals of the Founding Fathers. The founders fought the American Revolution against King George III for the right to determine their own government. Now the South was going to war against the North for that same right. Since the North denied the South's "right to self-government, refused even to listen to any proposals for a peaceful separation," nothing was left for the South to do but continue to wage war.[4]

The crowd erupted in loud applause and cheering. Davis waited for everyone to quiet down. People stood on the Capitol steps, roof, walkways, grass, and in windows, eager to hear their leader speak.

Davis continued his address. "To show ourselves worthy of the inheritance bequeathed to us by the patriots of the Revolution," the South must be

courageous and devoted to its cause.[5] Davis's eloquence convinced the crowd that Davis would return the South to the kind of government created by their forefathers.

After his speech, Judge James D. Halyburton administered the oath of office, and Jefferson Davis was proclaimed president of the Confederate States of America for a term of six years. Cries of "God bless our President" rumbled through the crowd as they slowly dispersed.

Davis had already served a year as provisional (temporary) president of the Confederacy. When Abraham Lincoln was elected president of the United States in November 1860, seven Southern states seceded from, or left, the Union. In February 1861, they held a convention in Montgomery,

Alabama, and formed the Confederate States of America. They drafted a temporary constitution, including an article recognizing the right to own slaves as property, and they

*This is Davis as he looked during his years as president of the Confederacy.*

unanimously chose Jefferson Davis to lead their new nation.

His job had been overwhelming. In addition to guiding the Confederacy through a civil war, he had to build a new nation. At first, the Confederate States had no government, little money, no army or navy, no postal system, few factories, and only a small number of railroad lines to transport food, supplies, and troops.

The Confederacy's first concern was a peaceful secession from the United States. Jefferson Davis agreed with most Southerners; they did not want war. A problem soon arose, however, over forts and Union property in the Southern states. Fort Sumter in Charleston Harbor, South Carolina, became the focus of the conflict.

Southerners did not want a Union presence in the heart of the Confederacy. Davis was prepared to compensate the United States for federal property in the Confederacy, including Fort Sumter. Lincoln, however, refused to deal with the Confederacy as a separate nation. Confederates were still Americans, he said—Americans in rebellion. Southerners felt they had no choice but to bombard the fort, and thus, the Civil War began.

Neither side was prepared for war. Northern volunteers signed up for ninety days. Lincoln thought the rebellion could be stamped out within three months. The plan was to take the Confederate capital, which had moved from Montgomery to Richmond, and put the Confederacy out of action. That did not happen for four years.

As a military man, Davis knew the war would last longer than three months. Southern volunteers signed up for twelve months. The South was fighting for independence from the North and to protect its homes and territory from Northern invaders. Though ill-equipped, Southerners had won most of the battles during the first year of war.

The odds of winning seemed stacked against the South from the beginning. There were twenty-three states in the Union versus eleven states in the Confederacy. The North had more men available to become soldiers. The South did have better generals to lead its armies. Southern soldiers were also skilled horsemen, and were familiar with the land where the war took place. Yet the South faced many more obstacles.

The North was industrialized and had factories to produce the arms and ammunition needed to carry on a war. The Southern economy was agrarian and had few factories to make military supplies. The South counted on foreign countries such as England and France to provide them. The plan was to sell the South's greatest asset, cotton, in exchange for war materials.

Lincoln prevented this by ordering a blockade on all Southern ports. The blockade cut off thirty-five

hundred miles of Southern coastline, crippling the Confederacy's efforts to raise money and buy arms and supplies. The Confederacy grew weaker as the blockade became more and more effective.

During the first year of war, the North was shocked by its losses. Lincoln began building an army to win future battles. With each additional defeat, the Union became more determined to teach the Confederates a lesson. By the time Davis took the oath of office as permanent president of the Confederacy, the South had suffered a few defeats, primarily in the West. A few days before the February 22 inauguration, the South lost Fort Donelson and Fort Henry in Tennessee.

Davis was frustrated by these losses, but he never gave up hope that the Confederacy would somehow gain back its territory and win independence from the North. That was not to be. By 1864, the Union armies had the upper hand, and the Confederates did not have enough manpower, supplies, and food to turn the tide. Although Davis refused to admit the war was lost, Confederate General Robert E. Lee finally surrendered in April 1865.

Although Jefferson Davis never achieved his dream of an independent Southern nation, the Civil War resulted in a stronger union of states than the Founding Fathers had planned in 1776 with one of the world's most stable governments.

# 2

# CHILDHOOD

Samuel and Jane Davis and their nine children lived in a four-room log cabin in southwestern Kentucky. The place was so crowded that when a tenth child was born on June 3, 1808, the Davises hoped he would be their last. Samuel was over fifty years old and Jane was nearly forty-seven. They named the baby Jefferson Finis Davis. The name Jefferson was in honor of Thomas Jefferson, the third president of the United States, one of Samuel's heroes. Finis means "final" in Latin, a language the well-educated Samuel Davis had studied. Jefferson was to be their final child.

Another child, born eight months later, also in a Kentucky log cabin, would have a great impact on

*This is the birthplace of Jefferson Davis at Fairview, Kentucky.*

Jefferson Davis's life. That child was Abraham Lincoln. When the two boys grew up, they would each become president, one of the United States and the other of the Confederate States of America.

When Jefferson Davis was two years old, his parents packed up their belongings and moved, taking along all their children except Joseph, the oldest, who stayed behind to study law in Hopkinsville, Kentucky. The rest of the family headed south along the Mississippi River into the Louisiana Territory. Samuel had heard about the rich land there and planned to start a farm. The land was fertile, but so were the mosquitoes. The annoying insects thrived in the Louisiana swamps, and sometimes brought a terrible disease—malaria.

After several years of fighting insects and struggling to survive, Samuel Davis moved his family to the Mississippi Territory. With the help of his sons and a few slaves, he cleared land and planted cotton. He built a cottage on a small hill covered with poplar trees and called it Poplar Grove. After Jane Davis planted rose gardens around the cottage, everyone called it Rosemont.

"Little Jeff" had a happy childhood at Rosemont. As the youngest child, he received a lot of attention and affection, particularly from his sisters. His brother Isaac taught him to fish and ride horses. When he was old enough, Isaac also taught him how to shoot, an important skill for those who lived on the frontier. Jeff was very close to his sister Polly, two years older than he. They played in the poplar groves and ran through the cotton fields. Sometimes they climbed trees in the orchard and picked fruit for the family.

## School Days

When Jeff was five or six, he started school in a log cabin about a mile from his home. After two years of basic education, Samuel wanted something better for his bright son. He decided the only way Jeff could get a first-rate education would be to leave the frontier. There were good schools in Kentucky where Jeff was born, and Samuel decided to send him there. Samuel chose the College of St. Thomas Aquinas, an academy run by the Catholic Church, which taught both younger and older students.

Jane Davis did not want her youngest child to be taken away from her. He was too young, she said, to go to a school seven hundred miles away. Also, she asked, how would a boy from a Baptist family get along with Roman Catholic teachings?

No matter how many arguments Jane made, Samuel insisted that their son had to leave home in order to get a decent education. When a friend of

*This is Rosemont, the home in Woodville, Mississippi, where Jefferson Davis grew up.*

Joseph's, Major Thomas Hinds, left for Kentucky with his family in May or early June 1816, Jeff went along.[1] He and the Hindses' son, Howell, were the same age and enjoyed riding their ponies through the wilderness.

Jeff had a great adventure traveling with the Hinds family. At night they ate dinner around a campfire, then slept under the stars. Sometimes they saw deer running in the woods and wild turkeys roosting on tree branches.

After traveling many days, they came to Nashville, Tennessee. There, Major Hinds visited his good friend, General Andrew Jackson. Jackson had become an American hero during the War of 1812. He was a gracious host and encouraged Jeff, Howell, and his son Andrew, Jr., to play together, ride their ponies, and have contests. The only thing he did not want them to do was wrestle because, he said, "to allow hands to be put on one another might lead to a fight."[2] Jeff remembered that for the rest of his life, and never spanked his children or hit his slaves.

Everyone had a good time at Jackson's home and hated to leave. However, the group finally headed for Kentucky's bluegrass country. On July 10, 1816, Jeff arrived at the College of St. Thomas Aquinas. He accomplished a lot in the two years he spent at the academy. He studied English and Latin grammar and learned to speak well. Most of all he acquired self-discipline and a respect for authority.

## Home Again

After two years at school, Jeff's mother insisted that he return home. This time he went by steamboat, the newest way to travel on the Ohio and Mississippi rivers. The trip was an adventure for Jeff. He saw Indians come down to the riverbanks to sell venison to the boat's captain, which the passengers ate for dinner. Whenever the boat tied up at settlements along the river, Jeff watched the roustabouts at work. He also watched the captain use a brass spyglass and bellow out orders.

When the steamboat finally landed at Natchez, Jeff's brothers, Joseph and Isaac, met him at the landing. They were surprised to see how much nine-year-old Jeff had grown. Joseph had to go back to his law office in town, so Isaac took Jeff home. They mounted their horses and headed for Rosemont, thirty-five miles away.

During the long ride, the brothers decided to play a trick on their mother. As they approached Rosemont, Jeff got off his horse and went ahead, trying to hide his excitement at being home again. When he saw his mother sitting on the veranda, he casually asked her if she had seen any stray horses. She played along, saying the only stray she had seen was her boy. Then she rushed down the stairs and hugged him.

Jeff expected a loving reception from his mother. She was always warm and affectionate. His father rarely showed any emotion toward his children, so his reaction to Jeff's homecoming surprised Jeff. Samuel was working in the fields with the slaves. When he saw his son, he took Jeff in his arms "with more emotion than I had ever seen him exhibit," Davis later recalled, "and kissed me repeatedly. I remember wondering why my father should have kissed so big a boy."[3]

Jeff attended local schools for the next five years, mainly the new Wilkinson County Academy. School was not his favorite place to be. He preferred riding horses or playing with his dogs. Once, when his teacher assigned what Jeff considered too much to memorize, he told the teacher there was no way he could learn all of it. The teacher refused to lighten the assignment, and the next day, Jeff was unprepared. When the teacher started to punish him, Jeff picked up his books and went home.

He told his father he no longer wished to go to school. His father calmly gave Jeff a choice: Either go back to school or work in the fields. Jeff remembered what good times he and Polly used to have running through the cotton fields, and chose the fields. He worked very hard from dawn until dusk alongside the slaves. After two days of exhausting cotton picking, Jeff decided school was not so bad after all. He went back and became a more serious student.

He enjoyed his early teen years at home. His father raised fine horses, and Jeff became a superb rider. He rode everywhere, even to visit his married sister Anna, who lived twenty-five miles away. She had moved to Louisiana. Their brother Benjamin, a doctor who also lived in Louisiana, brought his wife to Anna's home to meet his baby brother Jeff. The three Davises had a happy reunion.

Back home, Jeff liked to hunt in the woods and fish in the streams. During those years at Rosemont, he developed a strong moral character by observing his parents. His mother was kind and just, gentle and patient, honest and upright. And he never forgot what his father often told him: "[U]se every possible means to acquire useful knowledge as knowledge is power."[4]

## Transylvania University

By the spring of 1823, when Jeff was about to turn fifteen, his father felt that he had outgrown the county academy. Samuel arranged for Jeff to go back to Kentucky and enroll in Transylvania University at Lexington. Since Jeff wanted to be a lawyer like his brother Joseph, the school would be a good place to start.

The curriculum was tough. He studied languages, history, natural philosophy, mathematics, surveying, writing, and public speaking. Jeff became good at debating, a skill he would need as a lawyer.

Jefferson Davis developed into a serious student at Transylvania. He was, said a classmate,

> . . . a good student, always prepared with his lessons, very respectful and polite to the President and professors. I never heard him reprimanded for neglecting his studies, or for misconduct of any sort. . . . He was amiable, prudent, and kind to all with whom he was associated, and beloved by teachers and students.[5]

Because he was popular as well as a good student, at the end of his third year, sixteen-year-old Jeff was appointed one of eleven junior orators. He gave his first speech at the June 14, 1824, commencement. He spoke about friendship, and the Lexington *Monitor* reported, "Davis on 'Friendship' made friends of his hearers."[6]

That summer, Jeff's world turned upside down when Samuel Davis died of malaria on July 4, 1824. He was sixty-eight years old. "No son could have loved a father more tenderly," Jefferson Davis later wrote.[7] In a letter to his sister-in-law he said, "When I saw him last he told me we would probably never see each other again. Yet I still hoped to meet him once more, but Heaven has refused my wish."[8]

Joseph consoled his youngest brother and became like a father to him. He had arranged for Jeff to go to the United States Military Academy at West Point, New York. An appointment to West Point was a great honor, and Joseph had used his influence to secure it for his younger brother.

Jeff did not want to skip his senior year at Transylvania, nor did he wish to leave his friends. He had passed his exams with honors and was looking forward to the special privileges granted to seniors. He had never considered joining the military. He planned to study law at the University of Virginia after graduation.

Out of respect for his brother, Jeff agreed to try West Point for a year. Joseph promised him that he could then go to the University of Virginia if he did not like West Point.

## West Point

Jefferson Davis ended up spending four years at West Point. His record there was not particularly distinguished. The friends he chose tended to get into trouble. It was their way of rebelling against the strict military discipline. Students, called cadets, were told what time to get up; when to go to bed; how to clean their floors, make their beds, and wear their hair; and even what to wear.

Davis received a number of demerits for disobeying orders, not keeping his room clean, skipping chapel, and arriving late at drills (or missing them altogether!). His name also appeared on a list of cadets who were absent from quarters for long periods of time.

Where did he go? Most often to Benny Havens, a nearby tavern that served food and drinks. The

tavern was off-limits for cadets. Anyone caught there could be suspended from West Point.

Once, when Davis and a fellow cadet were having "a little frolic" at Benny Havens, someone told them a professor was coming.[9] Davis and his friend took a shortcut up a steep bank to get back to the barracks before they were discovered. His friend made it to the top of the bluff, but in his haste, Davis slipped and fell sixty feet down the riverbank. The professor never caught them, but Davis was so badly hurt that he spent four months in the hospital.

**Future Civil War Leaders at West Point**

West Point Military Academy on the Hudson River in New York trains officers for the United States Army. Among Davis's fellow cadets were men who would become future leaders, for both the North and the South, during the Civil War. *Robert E. Lee* became the commanding general of all Confederate troops. *Albert Sidney Johnston* was the man Davis regarded as the ablest Confederate general. *Joseph E. Johnston* caused Davis much irritation as a Confederate general. *John Magruder* was in the United States Army before the war and became a general in the Confederate Army. *Robert Anderson* was the Northern major in command of Fort Sumter when it was bombarded by the South in 1861.

Davis managed to stay out of trouble long enough to graduate from West Point in 1828. Academically, he was in the bottom third of his class, but he "attached no significance to class standing."[10] He considered it more important that he stood high in the opinion of his classmates. One cadet spoke glowingly of him: "Jefferson Davis was distinguished in the corps for his manly bearing, his high-toned and lofty character. His figure was very soldier-like and rather robust; his step springy, resembling the tread of an Indian 'brave' on the warpath."[11]

By the end of his four years at West Point, Davis had grown to his full height of five feet eleven inches. His golden-brown hair, blue-gray eyes, and finely chiseled features gave him a handsome, dignified appearance. He had gained the ramrod straight military posture that would stay with him for the rest of his life.

Before Davis entered West Point, he had not considered a military career. Gradually, he acquired a deep interest in military science. He told his sister, "The four years I remained at West Point made me a different creature from that which nature had designed me to be."[12] West Point had made him into a soldier, and Jefferson Davis was ready to begin his career.

# FRONTIER ARMY LIFE

After graduation from West Point, Brevet (temporary) Second Lieutenant Davis went home on leave to Rosemont. He had not been back for five years. His mother and sister, Lucinda Stamps, still lived in the old house, along with Lucinda's three daughters.

Davis also spent time with his oldest brother, Joseph, who had moved to his own plantation, called Hurricane. Though still a lawyer, Joseph spent most of his time raising cotton and livestock. Davis also visited Isaac and his family on their farm.

After three months of visiting with his family, Davis had to say good-bye to everyone except James Pemberton, the slave his father had given him.

Samuel Davis had presented each of his children with "a favorite slave when he or she left home."[1] James Pemberton had not been able to go to West Point with Davis, but accompanied Davis in 1828 as he headed off to begin his army career.

Army life was not as exciting as Davis had expected. Instead of leading soldiers into battle, he supervised the building of barracks and sawmills. Rather than marching off to war in exotic locations, he went on expeditions against unfriendly Indians along the western frontier.

In 1829, he took charge of repairing and enlarging Fort Crawford, a frontier post in the Michigan Territory. The fort needed to be strengthened and enlarged. Davis took a company of men and two guides in canoes up the Mississippi and Menominee rivers to the virgin forests 175 miles north of the fort. They set up a logging camp and began felling trees, cutting them into logs, tying them into rafts, and floating them downstream.

The work was not only tough, but also dangerous. One day they spotted a fleet of canoes gliding down the river. Davis and his men quickly hid in the woods and watched a group of Indians, wearing war paint and chanting war songs, skim past. From then on, Davis posted a guard to warn of approaching Indians. The guard also had to watch for wild animals, because the woods were full of black bears, deer, and elk.

Back at the fort, army life was dull and lonely. Davis again began to think about becoming a lawyer and ordered some beginning law books from New York. He eagerly read them and hoped that his next assignment would put him closer to a place where he could study law.

## Fort Winnebago

Unfortunately, his next posting was no closer to such benefits of civilization. In the autumn of 1829, Davis was assigned to Fort Winnebago, also in the Michigan Territory. Again, he was in charge of improving the fort. Sometimes he led expeditions against hostile Indians in the Northwest Territory (present-day Michigan and Wisconsin).

Several of Davis's classmates from West Point were also stationed at Fort Winnebago, so he did not feel as isolated as he had at Fort Crawford. He enjoyed racing his fellow officers on horseback. The men also passed time spearfishing on the river and fighting their dogs against wolves.[2] Davis had no interest in the most popular amusements at the fort—card games and gambling. Instead, he spent long hours reading.

He did, however, like going to the "gumbo balls" held by settlers in the region. These balls were named after the refreshments served: bowls of hot gumbo and freshly baked bread. Men brought their wives and daughters from miles around to dance to the lively tunes of a fiddler. Davis was a good dancer and very popular with the ladies.

## Davis Becomes Ill

In late July 1831, Davis received orders to build a sawmill on the Yellow River west of Fort Crawford. First he built a small fort and got acquainted with the local Indians, earning their respect by learning their language and customs. The chief liked him so much that he adopted Davis "within the sacred bond of brotherhood," and the Indians fondly called him "Little Chief."[3]

Davis worked very hard, standing for hours in the cold water to build the sawmill. He soon became ill with pneumonia. Had it not been for the tender care of his faithful slave, James Pemberton, he might have died on the western frontier. There were no hospitals, and the nearest doctor was days away. Still, Davis refused to take a medical leave until the sawmill was finished. He directed the work from his cot. He eventually recovered, but from then on, he battled illnesses off and on for the rest of his life.

After this crisis, Davis returned to Fort Crawford to oversee an enlargement of the fort. There, he faced a different kind of problem. He was twenty-three years old but looked nineteen. A brawny soldier boasted that he would not take orders from such a "baby-faced lieutenant."[4] When Davis explained how he wanted a certain part of the fort constructed, the soldier sneered, threatening him with a wood plank. Davis picked up a piece of wood and knocked the man down. The other soldiers shouted their approval of how Davis had stood up to this bully. He never had disciplinary problems again.

## Marriage

Fort Crawford was now under the command of Colonel Zachary Taylor. Taylor had brought his family with him, and Davis soon fell in love with Taylor's eighteen-year-old daughter, Sarah Knox Taylor. In the spring of 1833, he asked Colonel Taylor for Sarah's hand in marriage. Much to Davis's chagrin, Taylor said no. He did not want his daughters marrying soldiers. Taylor's wife and three daughters had always complained about his frequent absences and worried about his safety. Being a military wife was the last thing he wanted for Sarah.

For two years, Davis and Sarah continued to see each other secretly and wrote love letters back and forth. Finally Sarah gave her father an ultimatum. With or without his consent, she planned to marry the young lieutenant.

During their courtship, Davis worried about being able to provide for a wife on his low salary. He was nearly twenty-seven years old and had not saved much money in the seven years he had been with the army. To make matters worse, his chance of being promoted was not good because there were few vacant army posts. He did not want to give up his army officer's career, however.

Jefferson Davis took a leave of absence and went home to make up his mind about his future. He talked things over with his brother Joseph, who offered to give him eight hundred acres of land in Mississippi. Joseph also said he would lend Davis money to buy slaves to help clear the land. Davis could then make his living as a cotton planter.

Davis sent a letter of resignation to his commanding general at the War Department. It became effective on June 30, 1835.[5] By that time, he and Sarah Knox Taylor were married. The wedding took place in Louisville, Kentucky, on June 17, 1835, in the living room of Colonel Taylor's oldest sister, Elizabeth.[6]

After their marriage, the newlyweds moved to Hurricane, Joseph Davis's plantation, which had plenty of room for visiting relatives. Joseph's home had two main stories and a third that could house a dozen guests and their servants. The house, with indoor bathrooms and running water, seemed luxurious to Sarah, who had lived most of her life on frontier army posts with few comforts of civilization.

Davis, with the help of a dozen slaves, went to work clearing the land that Joseph had given him. Because the land was full of briers, Davis named his future plantation Brierfield. Summertime in the Mississippi Valley brought heat and mosquitoes. The mosquitoes were particularly bad that year, and some of them carried malaria. Both Davis and Sarah were infected with the disease.

When they did not respond to treatment, they took a boat down the Mississippi River to Bayou Sara in Louisiana. They hoped being on the higher ground would help them recover. Tragically, Sarah never recovered. She died on September 18, 1835.

It was more than a month before Davis was well enough to return to Hurricane. He was heartbroken, and greatly weakened by his illness. Joseph was so worried about him that he suggested that Davis go to Cuba for a while to regain his strength in the balmy tropical air. Wanting to get away from bad memories, Davis agreed.

Sarah's death changed Davis forever. Never again was he fun-loving and mischievous. Though devastated by his young wife's death, he learned to hide his emotions. From then on, no one ever saw his real feelings. He hid his grief behind a facade of self-control and great dignity and became serious about everything.

After returning to the United States, Davis spent a few weeks visiting friends in Washington, D.C. Some of his friends were involved in government, and he became very interested in politics.

## A New Life at Brierfield

Davis returned to Mississippi in the spring of 1836, still mourning his dead wife.[7] He settled down at

Brierfield and went to work turning the wilderness into a plantation. Within two years, he and his slaves had cleared the land, built a small house, planted oak groves and fig trees, and put in the first cotton crop.

Davis spent the next seven years managing his plantation. He had no reservations about owning and using slaves, an attitude he shared with most white Southerners. But he did not believe slaves should be beaten, as some slaveholders did. If a slave became ill or hurt, Davis provided him or her with proper health care. He even organized a court with slave juries to judge and punish misbehavior on the part of their fellow slaves.

During those years of seclusion at Brierfield, Davis became a voracious reader, reading mostly about history and government. He subscribed to several newspapers and followed national developments closely. Friends and neighbors noticed Davis's increasing interest in politics, and in December 1842, they selected him and Joseph to be delegates from Warren County to the Democratic State Convention. Jefferson Davis's political career was about to begin.

# 4

# POLITICS AND MARRIAGE

Now that Brierfield was a successful plantation and Davis part of the Southern aristocracy, he decided to give politics a try. Instead of joining the Whigs, the party that dominated politics in his Mississippi voting district, Davis became a Democrat. The Democratic party believed that state governments should play a leading role in building roads and making other improvements. They were against centralized federal power and the idea of a national bank. Whigs, on the other hand, supported a strong federal government and a national bank to control finances from one central location.

In 1843, Davis, age thirty-five, ran for a seat in the Mississippi legislature. Although he lost, he gained name recognition as well as the attention of state Democratic leaders. In addition to his talent for public speaking and his command of political issues, people were impressed with his poise, his tall and erect military bearing, and the quiet dignity with which he conducted himself.

Davis also made an impression that year on Varina Banks Howell, the daughter of friends who lived in nearby Natchez, Mississippi. In December, Joseph Davis invited Varina to Hurricane for a Christmas party. Varina was flattered that Jefferson Davis paid so much attention to her. She thought he was handsome and very dignified, with fine manners and a soft, mellow voice.

In a letter to her mother, Varina said Davis was "a remarkable kind of man, but of uncertain temper, and has a way of taking for granted that everyone agrees with him when he expresses an opinion, which offends me."[1] (This quality would also offend others in the future.)

Although Varina was only seventeen years old, Davis was struck by her maturity. She could discuss literature, law, and politics with intelligence. She was bright and independent, and he found her attractive—tall with dark hair and a good figure. He was especially pleased that she was such a fine horsewoman. They rode around Hurricane every day, and Davis took her to see Brierfield.

By the time Varina returned home, she and Davis had fallen in love. He found Hurricane dull without her, and thought of her constantly.[2] She wrote how much she loved and missed him, and enclosed in her letters mementos such as a pressed flower she had worn or a lock of her hair. He kept these treasures in a secret hiding place.

In the middle of March, Davis went to Natchez to ask Varina's parents for permission to marry her. They said yes, and the engagement was announced. However, Varina and Davis did not marry for nearly a year because he was so involved in politics.

Between political activities, Davis dashed to Natchez to see Varina. Both were happy when Democrat James K. Polk won the presidential election in November 1844. They felt they could finally get on with their lives. Davis and Varina were married at her home on February 26, 1845. They took a six-week honeymoon, visiting Davis's eighty-three-year-old mother on their way to New Orleans. Then they settled down at Brierfield.

## Davis Becomes a Congressman

The Davises enjoyed a few months of peaceful plantation life. Then, in July, the state Democratic party nominated Davis for a seat in the United States House of Representatives. In November, he was elected to his first term in Congress.

Varina was happy for her husband because she knew how much he loved politics. She looked

*Thirty-six-year-old Jefferson Davis met seventeen-year-old Varina Howell at his brother Joseph's Christmas party in 1843. Despite the age difference, they fell in love and married in February 1845.*

forward to an exciting life in Washington. Davis, age thirty-seven, began training James Pemberton to take care of Brierfield and oversee the slaves during his absence. The number of slaves Davis owned had multiplied from twelve to seventy-four.[3]

As soon as they moved to Washington, Davis went to work. Normally, first-term congressmen kept quiet, observing and learning from their more experienced colleagues. But Davis made a speech ten days after taking office. The reaction was so favorable that one reporter wrote, "Jefferson Davis earned a wreath of fame" with his speech.[4]

Davis's next speech was about Oregon. Since 1818, the United States and Great Britain had occupied the Oregon Territory jointly. By the 1840s, so many American emigrants had moved to the territory that there was increasing talk about ousting the British and annexing Oregon, making it part of the United States.

Extremists thought the country should go to war against Great Britain to gain this territory. But Davis spoke of annexing only the part of the territory where emigrants had settled—to the 49th parallel on the map. That would leave the rest of Oregon for the British, and lessen the chance of war. He asked his fellow congressmen if they would "allow Britain to occupy all of Oregon without a fight? Of course not. . . . Given the option of part of Oregon with peace, or all of it," which might result in war with Britain, he knew he would choose peace.[5]

Varina Davis was in the visitors' gallery when he spoke, and she sat "enthralled" as she heard the warm applause given to Davis after his speech. She was very proud of her husband.[6]

## War with Mexico

At the same time as the dispute over Oregon, the United States was disputing its boundary with Mexico. In 1836, Texas had broken off from Mexico and declared itself the "Lone Star Republic."[7] In 1845, Texas asked to join the United States. When Congress approved the request, the Mexican

**"54-40 or Fight"**

This was a slogan used during the boundary dispute between the United States and Great Britain over Oregon. Under an 1818 treaty, both nations had agreed to jointly occupy the area lying between 42° and 54°40' north latitude. In the 1840s, many emigrants traveled west in wagon trains along the Oregon Trail and settled in the Willamette Valley (around present-day Portland). Expansionists talked about going to war against England to gain the entire area. Cooler heads prevailed, however, and a new treaty in 1846 set the United States boundaries between 42° and 49° north latitude. The British obtained the territory above the line. This later became Canada.

government severed relations with the United States.

Mexico did not recognize Texan independence, nor did it acknowledge the Rio Grande as the state's southern boundary, as Texas claimed. Mexican troops periodically crossed the Rio Grande to show that the territory still belonged to Mexico.

In August 1845, General Zachary Taylor moved a small force of troops to Corpus Christi, on the Nueces River. After repeated attempts to settle the boundary dispute through diplomacy, President

Polk ordered Taylor's troops to the Rio Grande to establish the United States border.

Tension between the United States and Mexico reached a breaking point. On May 11, 1846, Congress declared war on Mexico, and Polk asked the states to organize volunteer regiments to fight in the war. The United States Army was small, so the government employed volunteers to fight wars.

Although Davis had been in Congress for less than six months, he believed it was his patriotic duty to fight for his country. He wrote a letter to the Vicksburg *Sentinel*, promoting the war with Mexico. Then he promoted himself by saying his West Point education and prior military service qualified him to lead the Mississippi regiment. The editor of the *Sentinel* wrote in bold letters, **"Major Davis Is the Man!"** and suggested that Mississippi volunteers elect him, a "native, gallant, glorious son of our soil."[8]

In late June, Davis was elected colonel and commander of the 1st Mississippi Infantry Regiment. He accepted the appointment and resigned from Congress.

Varina Davis was not happy that her husband had volunteered to go to war and worried about his safety. Davis assured her that he would be fine.

They left Washington on July 4, 1846. Davis stayed one night at Brierfield, just long enough to put his affairs in order. Then he left on horseback for New Orleans, where the Mississippi regiment had gathered.

The regiment of nine hundred volunteers greeted Davis enthusiastically when he arrived on July 21. On July 26, they sailed for southern Texas on the *Alabama*. A week later, they set up camp near the mouth of the Rio Grande.

Davis put the men through strenuous drills under the blazing Texas sun. They had rifle practice with the new Whitney rifles he had ordered from Washington before he left. The regiment became known as the Mississippi Rifles because they were the first to use these new firearms.[9]

After only three weeks of training, the regiment crossed the Rio Grande into Mexico and joined General Zachary Taylor's troops. Most of Taylor's regular army had been sent south to join General Winfield Scott's troops, because Scott needed a large force to take Mexico City. Taylor stayed behind with mostly volunteer troops to keep northern Mexico in American hands. Mexican General Antonio López de Santa Anna saw that the United States Army was divided and that his troops outnumbered Taylor's troops four to one. He decided to chase Taylor's troops back across the border.

Thanks to Taylor's courage and the brave fighting of Davis and the Mississippi Rifles, that did not happen. During the Battle of Buena Vista on February 22, 1847, Davis was shot in the foot, but

*Jefferson Davis is shown here wearing his Army of Mississippi uniform.*

he continued to lead his troops. He devised a brilliant strategy that held the Mexicans at bay, enabling Taylor to win an impressive victory over Santa Anna.

News of this victory won national praise for both Taylor and Davis. Taylor became such a popular figure that he would soon be elected president. Davis was called "the hero of Buena Vista" and became the pride of Mississippi.[10] He went home on crutches with his regiment in June 1847, when their one-year term of enlistment ended. In September of that year, Davis was delighted to hear that American troops had captured Mexico City. The war came to an end in early 1848.

## Senator Davis

The Mississippi legislature unanimously chose Davis to fill a vacant United States Senate seat in December 1847. Davis was back in Washington, now a national hero. The next year, Mississippi voters elected him to a full six-year term.

Everyone was talking about the annexation of the newly won Mexican territory. Davis wanted the United States to annex all of the territory, but in the end, only the land above the Rio Grande was annexed, as well as all the land west to the Pacific Ocean.

Adding these territories to the United States raised heated debate over the question of slavery. Northern states wanted to exclude slavery from new territories, including Oregon. Southern states said that if slavery were excluded from the new territories when they became states, there would no longer be an equal number of slave states and free states. Once there was a three-fourths majority of free states in Congress, they could amend the Constitution and abolish slavery forever (if the states ratified it).

**Missouri Compromise**

In 1820, a compromise was reached whereby Missouri was admitted to the Union as a slave state and Maine was admitted as a free state. This preserved the balance of power in Congress between the slave and free states. The compromise also stated that from then on, Congress would admit no more slave states north of 36°30', the parallel of latitude that marked Missouri's southern boundary.

Davis and others believed the Southern way of life would be destroyed. Because land in the South was very fertile, crops such as cotton, rice, and tobacco were grown on small farms and large plantations. As cotton plantations spread across the South, cotton became the largest source of American revenue. A large workforce was needed to cultivate the fields, and slaves provided a cheap source of labor.

The industrialized North did not need slaves to work in manufacturing and trade. There, factories had replaced agriculture as the main source of income, and immigrants provided a ready labor force. Some Northerners thought slavery was wrong and demanded that Congress enact laws against it.

Davis believed the Southern states had the right to run their state governments the way that best suited them. In a speech before the Senate, he said that if Congress ignored the South's rights, "We should part peaceably and avoid staining the battlefields of the Revolution with the blood of civil war."[11]

## Growing Conflict

The discovery of gold in California in 1848 brought thousands of emigrants into California Territory. In 1850, the territorial legislature asked Congress to make California a state. At that time, there were fifteen free and fifteen slave states. Admitting California to the Union would upset that balance.

**States' Rights**

In the years before the Civil War, the nation was divided over the issue of what rights and powers the states possessed as opposed to the federal government. Southerners believed that all powers not specifically given to the federal government by the Constitution belonged to the states. This included the right to end the partnership formed in 1788 when the thirteen original states ratified the Constitution.

No issue was more important to Jefferson Davis than states' rights. He said the states had, of their own free will, entered into a contract with the federal government to provide certain services. By virtue of the same free will, states could withdraw from the contract if they were not satisfied with how the government was doing its job.

Senator Henry Clay, with the help of Senators Daniel Webster and Stephen A. Douglas, crafted a compromise to defuse the situation. Called the Compromise of 1850, the plan called for California to be admitted to the Union as a free state and the rest of the newly won territory to be organized without restrictions on slavery. The people in the territories would decide for themselves whether to allow slavery.

Davis led an unsuccessful fight in the Senate to defeat the Compromise of 1850. He felt the bill did

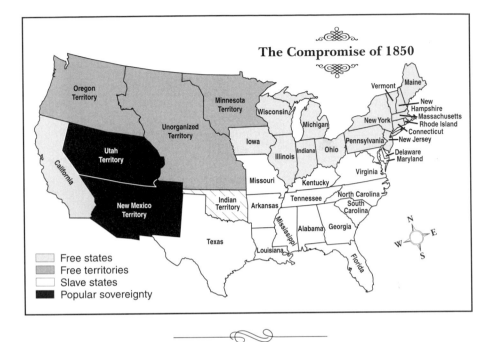

### The Compromise of 1850

Free states
Free territories
Slave states
Popular sovereignty

*The Compromise of 1850 was designed to prevent conflict in determining whether new states being admitted to the Union would be slave or free. This map shows how the different areas of the United States were affected.*

not protect the rights of Southern states. More moderate Southerners, however, were willing to compromise to preserve the Union, and the bill passed. The South was not yet ready to secede.

In 1851, Davis resigned from the Senate to run for governor of Mississippi. During the campaign, Davis spoke out for states' rights. Davis narrowly lost the election and returned home to Brierfield, disillusioned with politics.

# 5

# SPOKESMAN FOR THE SOUTH

Davis settled into plantation life. He and his wife worked together in the garden, planting rosebushes, oak saplings, and an orchard of fruit trees. Their new house, which had taken four years to build, was almost finished, and they were finally able to move in.

After seven years of marriage, the Davises were thrilled to become parents. They named their son Samuel after Jefferson Davis's father. The slaves were given the day off and they had a grand celebration. They came to the house with gifts for the baby—a newly laid egg, a baby chick, a wildflower bouquet, a sweet potato grown in one of their little gardens.

The same year young Samuel Davis was born, Harriet Beecher Stowe, a Northern writer, published a novel that caused a sensation in both the North and the South. *Uncle Tom's Cabin* told a story about the mistreatment of Southern slaves. Northerners read the book and believed all slaves were treated cruelly. Southerners who thought they treated their slaves well were angry. Jefferson Davis said the publication of such an inflammatory book added to the agitation between the North and the South.[1]

## Secretary of War

In 1852, Democrat Franklin Pierce was elected president and asked Davis to be his secretary of war. Varina begged her husband not to accept, but he could not turn down a prestigious Cabinet position. He was well qualified for the job and knew how to get things done in the United States government. As secretary of war, Davis earned a reputation for being honest, incorruptible, and hardworking.

Because of his military experience, he knew how to improve the nation's armed forces. Using the latest technological advances from Europe, he modernized the United States Army. He set up a system to manufacture, repair, and stock arms, munitions, and war material. He also built armories (weapon storehouses) in strategic sections of the country, including the Pacific Coast. He even secured a pay increase for enlisted men.[2]

*This portrait of Jefferson Davis was done while he was secretary of war under President Franklin Pierce.*

Between 1853 and 1857, the four years he served as secretary of war, many emigrants were moving west. They settled on Indian homelands. When the Indians fought to keep their territory, Davis sent army troops to subdue them and negotiate peace treaties. To make the region safe for settlement, he set up a network of more than sixty frontier forts.

## Davis Gains a Family

The worst event that happened to Davis at this time was the death of his son. Samuel became ill and died on June 30, 1854, just one month before his second birthday.[3] Davis did not show his grief, because, above all else, he believed in self-control. But Varina wrote to her father that Davis "walked half the night and worked fiercely all day" and that "a child's crying in the street would cause him acute distress."[4]

Fortunately, daughter Margaret was born in February 1855. Two years later, in January 1857, a

son named Jefferson, Jr., arrived. In April 1859, another son, Joseph, was born. While these children could never take the place of his firstborn son, Davis enjoyed his family. They took his mind off "the burdens and irritations of official business."[5] He spent many happy hours playing with his children.

## Turmoil in Kansas

While Davis was a member of President Pierce's Cabinet, conflict between the North and the South heated up again. This time the focus was on the Kansas and Nebraska territories. In 1854, Stephen Douglas, a prominent senator from Illinois, proposed his popular sovereignty plan to end the dispute. His plan would repeal the Missouri Compromise, which had set boundaries for the spread of slavery, and let the settlers in new territories decide for themselves whether or not they wanted slavery. After a fierce congressional debate, Douglas's plan was passed as the Kansas-Nebraska Act. Immediately a struggle began to see who would control Kansas.

The Kansas prairie became a war zone. People were ambushed, kidnapped, and even killed. Both sides were guilty of outrageous crimes. Davis sent in the army to enforce the law. Still, skirmishes continued to break out. In 1856, a fanatical abolitionist (antislavery) settler named John Brown decided to take the law into his own hands. He and four of his sons raided two cabins of Southern settlers and stabbed five men to death.

Much of this turmoil took place during 1856, an election year. People began to mention Davis's name as a candidate for vice president of the United States. Davis was not interested. He told friends, "I would not have an office which, however dignified, affords no sphere for the display of administrative talent or powers in debate."[6] He preferred, he said, to be a candidate for the next available Senate seat from Mississippi. The Mississippi legislature was

**Popular Sovereignty**

Popular sovereignty was a concept in the 1850s that said the people in each new territory should be able to decide for themselves prior to statehood whether they wanted to be a free state or a slave state. The idea was ambiguous enough to appeal to both Northerners and Southerners. It also avoided problems with the 1820 Missouri Compromise, which limited slavery in the Louisiana Territory to the area south of latitude 36°30', the southern boundary of Missouri. The boundary line stood until 1854 when Senator Stephen A. Douglas invoked popular sovereignty in his Kansas-Nebraska Act. This act repealed the Missouri Compromise and opened the territories to slavery.

happy to nominate Davis for its vacant Senate seat, and Davis was elected by a landslide.

## Another Term as Senator

Davis took his Senate seat on March 4, 1857, the day his Cabinet position expired. Two days later, the *Dred Scott* decision came down from the Supreme Court. Dred Scott was a Missouri slave whose master took him to Illinois, a free state, and Wisconsin, a free territory, in 1834. Four years later Scott returned to Missouri, a slave state, with his master. Scott felt that because he had lived in areas where slavery was illegal, he could no longer be held as a slave. In 1846, he sued his owner for his freedom.

The Supreme Court justices ruled against Scott's claim for freedom, concluding that a slave was private property and that the Constitution protected a citizen's private property. They also said Congress had no power to prohibit slavery in any part of the United States, which meant that the Missouri Compromise was unconstitutional, and therefore void. The *Dred Scott* decision enraged abolitionists, who vowed to continue their crusade against the expansion of slavery.

The atmosphere in the Senate grew increasingly bitter. Northern and Southern senators made hostile speeches against each other's views. For his part, Davis tried to avoid the topic of slavery and was thankful when the first session of Congress ended.

### Violence on the Senate Floor

In May 1856, Senator Charles Sumner of Massachusetts gave a speech in which he attacked South Carolina for its role in the fight over whether Kansas would become a free or slave state. Sumner also made hateful remarks against South Carolina's senior senator, Andrew P. Butler, who was not present. Three days later, South Carolina Congressman Preston Brooks, Butler's cousin, entered the Senate holding a cane, walked over to Sumner's seat, told him his speech had slandered both South Carolina and his relative, then beat Sumner on the head and shoulders with the cane until it broke.

Because of the incident, Brooks had to resign from the House of Representatives. However, he became such a hero in his home state that he was reelected in the next election. People from all over the South sent him new canes, some inscribed with phrases like "Hit Him Again" and "Use Knock-Down Arguments."[7]

## Back in Mississippi

In May 1857, Davis and his family returned to their Mississippi plantation. Davis was glad to be home. Everywhere he went, people crowded around to meet him. Davis sought the viewpoints of all his constituents.

Davis made speeches around the state, talking about the rights of Southerners to own slaves and

how the government must protect slaves in the territories just as it protected all other private property. He also tried to get answers to a question he was struggling with. Would Southerners, though the majority of them did not own slaves, agree to secede from the Union if they felt slavery was threatened?

## Spokesman for the South

The Senate reconvened on December 7, 1857. On December 8, the first item on the agenda was whether to admit Kansas as a free state or a slave state. A proslavery constitution had been drawn up, voted on, and approved by a minority of settlers in the territory. President James Buchanan asked Congress to admit Kansas as a slave state. Senator Stephen A. Douglas spoke out against it.

Davis and other Southerners were shocked because it was Douglas who had introduced the idea of "popular sovereignty," which let the territories decide for themselves whether or not to allow slaves. Davis realized that Douglas was trying to please Northern voters. He wanted to be president and hoped to be nominated in the 1860 election. By opposing Buchanan on the Kansas situation, Douglas made Northern Democrats sit up and take notice. (Southern Democrats like Davis took notice, too.) By this action Douglas created a rift in the Democratic party that would be disastrous in the next election.

Davis continued to speak out about the rights of states to decide the slavery issue. He became the acknowledged spokesman for the South. Horace Greeley, an antislavery editor of the New York *Tribune*, wrote:

> Mr. Davis is unquestionably the foremost man of the South today. Every Northern Senator will admit that from the southern side of the floor the most formidable to meet in debate is the thin, polished, intellectual-looking Mississippian . . . [8]

The pressure of the North-South antagonism strained Davis's health. He caught a severe cold, then nerve spasms and extreme pain attacked one side of his face. His left eye became so inflamed and swollen he thought it would burst. For a time, doctors feared they would have to remove the eye. Fortunately, that did not happen, but because Davis could stand no light, he lay for weeks in a darkened room. Friends visited and told him what was happening in the Senate.

Gradually, he recovered, and by late 1858, he was able to return to the Senate. Fighting the same battles as before, Davis spoke out more strongly than ever for states' rights and the expansion of slavery into the territories. He spoke out against the Republicans, whom he believed were attempting to take control of the government for the purpose of abolishing slavery.

In 1859, civil strife heated up, with both sides making ever more dire threats. Americans became deeply divided over how to resolve their differences. Then, in October, abolitionist John Brown, who had already killed five men in Kansas, decided it was time to act. He and an armed band of thirteen white men and five blacks seized the federal arsenal at Harpers Ferry, Virginia. His plan was to arm the slaves and lead them in a revolt against their masters. Brown's plan failed, and he was imprisoned, tried, and hanged.

John Brown's raid ended any hope that the North and the South could settle their differences. Slaveholders feared the North was planning more invasions of the South. The Senate appointed a committee of five to investigate Brown's actions. As a member of the committee, Davis became frustrated when Northern senators tried to condemn slavery rather than work on a plan to prevent more actions like Brown's.

Davis realized he had to do something to protect slavery, especially in the new territories. He drew up a series of resolutions to protect Southern rights. One resolution said no citizen had the right to meddle in the affairs of another state. Another held that the government must guarantee the rights of slaveholders in the territories until the population applied for statehood and decided the slavery issue for itself. After much discussion in the Senate, the Davis resolutions passed in May 1860.

These were only resolutions, not laws. Still, they served to emphasize the South's strong feelings about slaveholder rights. Davis was looking ahead to the upcoming presidential election. He knew he would not be a candidate. His support of Southern rights was considered too radical for him to get enough Northern votes to win in the general election. Yet he wanted Northern Democrats to be aware that in order to win they must nominate a candidate who would be sympathetic to Southern issues.

## 1860 Elections

The increasing tension between the North and the South had a dramatic effect on the Democratic and Republican national conventions in 1860. The Democrats, unable to agree on a candidate, split three ways. The Northern wing of the party nominated Stephen A. Douglas of Illinois. The Southern wing selected Senator John C. Breckinridge of Kentucky. Remnants of the old Whig party plus members of minor parties nominated John Bell of Tennessee.

Davis realized that the Democratic party would be defeated in the November elections if it remained split. He suggested that the nominated candidates withdraw from the race so that Democrats could choose a single compromise candidate. Douglas refused. He had wanted to be president for years and believed he could win.

Unlike the Democrats, the Republicans agreed on a compromise candidate. Everyone had expected William Seward, head of the Republican party, to get

the nomination. Various delegates, however, were committed to three other candidates, and Seward came up sixty votes short of getting the nomination on the first ballot. Abraham Lincoln was everyone's second choice, and his colleagues stirred up support for him. After three ballots, Lincoln won the nomination.

Lincoln was a moderate on the slavery question, and Northerners hoped the South would accept him if he were elected. While Lincoln agreed that the Constitution forbade presidential action against slavery where it already existed, he pledged to halt the further spread of slavery into the territories.

That was unacceptable to the South. Senator John J. Crittenden of Kentucky said the South "has come to the conclusion that in case Lincoln should be elected . . . she could not submit to the consequences, and therefore, to avoid her fate, will secede from the Union."[9]

These were strong words, but Lincoln did not think the South would follow through on its threats. Disunion would ruin the country, and he was sure no one wanted that.

Lincoln won the election, and Northerners celebrated the triumph of antislavery. Southerners reacted to the 1860 election as strongly as colonists in 1773 had reacted to the British Tea Act. Referring to the Boston Tea Party, the Charleston *Mercury* wrote, "The tea has been thrown overboard; the revolution of 1860 has been initiated."[10] Secession was inevitable.

# 6

# CONFEDERATE PRESIDENT

On December 20, 1860, South Carolina seceded from the United States. Within six weeks, Mississippi, Florida, Alabama, Georgia, Louisiana, and Texas also had withdrawn from the Union. Jefferson Davis realized the consequences of such actions. If the two sides could not resolve their problems, it would be a catastrophe. He reminded everyone that the Southern states hoped for a peaceful separation from the Union.

The South had no intention of invading the North, he said, and he implored the North not to make war against the South. He asked that the North just let the South go in peace.

With his military background, Davis realized the South was not prepared for war. For the past year, Davis had been helping the governor of Mississippi arm the state with new and modern weapons. But Davis feared the rest of the South was not as forward-looking.

The stress of trying to curb the passions of both sides took a toll on his health. His facial pain almost blinded him, and he spent a week in bed. He tried to carry on business anyway, mainly by writing letters. South Carolina Governor Francis Pickens had written to Davis with some startling news. A Northern supply ship had attempted to take men and supplies to Fort Sumter in Charleston Harbor, South Carolina. The Union insisted that Fort Sumter was federal property, even though it was in Southern territory. South Carolina militia fired on the supply ship and drove it away. Governor Pickens asked Davis for military advice.

Davis told him not to demand surrender of the fort because it posed no immediate danger to the South. "We are probably soon to be involved in that fiercest of human strife, a civil war," Davis said.[1] The South should not start any conflict until it was prepared.

## Davis Resigns from the Senate

On January 21, 1861, Davis made his farewell speech to the Senate. Word had spread that he would be speaking there for the last time in his distinguished career. The place was jammed with congressmen, their wives, and as many other spectators as could squeeze into the chamber. Varina Davis sat in the gallery and wondered if anyone in the crowd would notice her husband's "deep depression, his desire for reconciliation, and his overweening love for the Union."[2]

Davis began by explaining why he was leaving. He agreed with the people of Mississippi that "[W]e are to be deprived in the Union of the rights which our fathers bequeathed to us."[3] Secession was both "necessary and proper," he explained. It was "justified upon the basis that the States are sovereign. There was a time when none denied it. I hope the time may come again. . . ."[4]

He went on to say that he hoped for peaceful and friendly relations even though the North and South must part. After bidding everyone in the chamber "a final adieu," Davis sat down, sapped of all his remaining strength.[5] The applause was thunderous and there were tears in many eyes.

## Back in Mississippi

The Davis family left Washington on a train bound for Mississippi. Varina, age thirty-four, and the Davis children were eager to see their plantation again. Davis, age fifty-two, looked forward to going back to Brierfield, too, although he knew it would not be for long. He thought about the letter he had

just received from South Carolina Governor Pickens:

> What we [the seceded states] want is, as soon as the states can meet at Montgomery, Alabama, for them to elect immediately a Commander-in-Chief for the States and assess the States their quota in army and men and money. . . . Allow me to say that I think you are the proper man to be selected at this juncture . . .[6]

Davis had already been appointed to the position of major general of the Army of Mississippi by the governor of Mississippi. He preferred this new job to the possible position mentioned by Pickens.

When the Davis family reached Jackson, they stayed for a few days while Davis began organizing the state's militia and making provision for arms and ammunition. He was dismayed by how ill-prepared for war Mississippi was and hoped the North and South could still solve their differences peacefully.

The family finally arrived at Brierfield in late January. While the Davises were enjoying the peace and quiet of country life, delegates from the seven seceded states were meeting in Montgomery, Alabama, to form a new government. On February 8, 1861, they drafted a Confederate constitution and chose Jefferson Davis as provisional president.

On February 10, Jefferson and Varina Davis were pruning their rosebushes when a messenger on horseback galloped up with a telegram. Davis read the telegram, and from the look on his face, his wife thought something terrible had happened. After a painful silence, Davis told her he had been elected president of the Confederacy. But, she wrote, he said it "as a man might speak of a sentence of death."[7]

Davis had hoped to be commander of the South's army in case of war. With a heavy heart, he accepted the presidency out of a sense of duty. The next day he said good-bye to his wife and children and left for Alabama.

## President of the Confederacy

It took Davis six days to reach Montgomery. On the way he made twenty-five speeches, thanking the people for their enthusiastic welcome and assuring them that the South had no choice left but to stand up for its rights.

When the train reached Montgomery, cannons fired a salute to Davis and enthusiastic crowds cheered for him. Bands played "Dixie," the new, unofficial Southern anthem. In a brief speech at the train station, Davis told the large crowd,

> We [will] maintain our right to self-government at all hazards. We ask nothing, want nothing, and will have no complications. If other States should desire to join our Confederation, they can freely come on our terms. Our separation from the old Union is complete.[8]

The next morning, February 18, 1861, Jefferson Davis took the oath of office as provisional president of the Confederate States of America. (The position

was a temporary one. An election would be held in November to select the permanent president.)

Davis then went to work organizing the Confederacy. In an attempt to unite the new government, he chose a man from each seceded state to be one of his official advisors. These men made up his Cabinet. He also began drawing up war plans and organizing production of war materials for an invasion he hoped would never come. Davis felt being prepared would best protect peace.

In another attempt to prevent war, Davis named a peace commission to go to Washington, D.C., after Lincoln's inauguration to discuss ways the two sides could coexist. Davis was especially interested in transferring Fort Sumter in Charleston Harbor to the Confederacy. Charleston, South Carolina, was one of the Confederacy's most important harbors, and they could not allow an enemy fort in the middle of it.

Davis also worked hard to persuade the eight slave states still in the Union (Virginia, North Carolina, Tennessee, Arkansas, Maryland, Kentucky, Missouri, and Delaware) to join the Confederacy. The bigger and stronger the Confederacy, he believed, the better its chance for success. The states of the Upper South (Virginia, Arkansas, North Carolina, and Tennessee) had resisted secession. They preferred to wait until they saw what Lincoln would do after he took office.

Abraham Lincoln was inaugurated on March 4, 1861, in Washington, D.C. He took the oath of office, pledging to occupy and protect all federal property, including that in the South. In his inaugural speech he addressed the slavery issue, promising not to interfere with the institution where it already existed. But he also said he believed no state had the right to secede from the Union. That was an act of rebellion against the United States that could not be allowed.

## Fort Sumter

Lincoln stood firm on his pledge to protect federal property and refused to turn over Fort Sumter to Confederate South Carolina. When he received word that the seventy-nine Union troops stationed in the fort were running short of supplies, he decided to send provisions to them. But before sending a supply ship, he informed Governor Pickens that he was sending only nonmilitary supplies. Furthermore, he said he would not reinforce or rearm the fort as long as South Carolina did not attack the fort or the supply ships.

As part of their war preparations, the Confederates had positioned guns and mortars on three sides of Fort Sumter, aimed at the Union guns mounted inside the fort. When Davis learned that a fleet of Union ships was approaching the fort, he realized that negotiations with the North for the

**Border States**

Delaware, Maryland, Missouri, and Kentucky were slave states on the border between the North and the South. President Lincoln was determined to keep these states in the Union, and he used a combination of delicate handling and hardfisted ruthlessness to keep them from joining the Confederacy. Delaware remained loyal to the Union despite having strong Southern sentiments. Maryland was occupied by Northern troops to keep it in the Union. Both pro-Union and pro-Confederate governments were established in Missouri, and the state was plagued by brutal guerrilla warfare throughout the war. It did not leave the Union, although its pro-South governor established a Confederate government in exile. Kentucky tried to remain neutral and thus was given delicate consideration by Lincoln.

transfer of Fort Sumter to the Confederacy had failed. There was nothing to do but take it by force.

Davis sent a telegram to the Confederate commander at Charleston, General Pierre G. T. Beauregard, telling him to demand that the Union soldiers surrender Fort Sumter. In the predawn hours of April 12, 1861, three of Beauregard's aides rowed out to the fort to deliver the message: Surrender or the guns ringing the harbor will fire on the fort.

The Union commander, Major Robert Anderson, refused to surrender. On April 12, 1861, at 4:30 A.M., Beauregard's men opened fire. After thirty-four hours of bombardment, the Union forces, badly outnumbered, sent up a white flag and surrendered.

No person on either side was killed during the shelling, only a mule. Davis was thankful and still hoped for peace. "Separation is not yet of necessity final—there has been no blood spilled more precious than that of a mule," he said.[9]

The North wanted revenge. The shelling of Fort Sumter was an act of war. Lincoln immediately

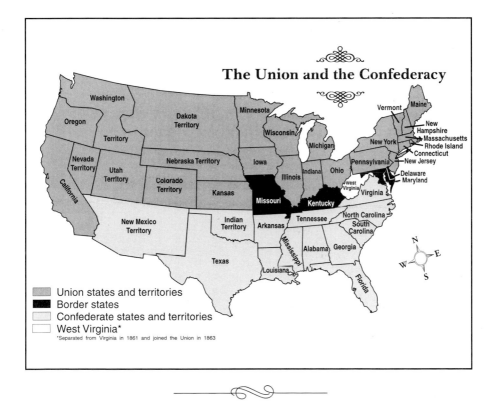

### The Union and the Confederacy

Union states and territories
Border states
Confederate states and territories
West Virginia*
*Separated from Virginia in 1861 and joined the Union in 1863

*This map shows how the states were divided in their loyalties to the Union or the Confederacy.*

*A Confederate flag flies over Fort Sumter on April 14, 1861, after a thirty-four-hour bombardment by Confederate gunners forced the Union to withdraw.*

issued a proclamation calling for seventy-five thousand militiamen. Then it was the South's turn to be angry. Four more states seceded: Virginia, Arkansas, Tennessee, and North Carolina. Davis's hopes for a peaceful resolution were dashed, and he called for one hundred thousand volunteers.

The Civil War had begun.

# 7

# CIVIL WAR

The bombardment of Fort Sumter produced bursts of patriotism throughout the North and the South. In New York's Union Square, a crowd of one hundred thousand New Yorkers massed in the square, demanding vengeance.

Upon hearing that Virginia had seceded, a procession marched around the capital at Richmond. In Wilmington, North Carolina, Confederate flags flew from every public building. Throughout the South, whenever new volunteers passed through railroad stations, women and girls waited on the platform to cheer them on, waving handkerchiefs. In Alabama, trains full of volunteers on their way to

Montgomery were greeted by torchlight parades as they moved through towns.

Mary Chesnut, who kept a diary during the Civil War, wrote about the first few months after Fort Sumter:

> **July 4, 1861:** Noise of drums, tramp of marching regiments all day long, rattling of artillery wagons, bands of music, friends from every quarter coming in. We ought to be miserable and anxious, and yet these are pleasant days.[1]

Presidents Lincoln and Davis did not think the days were so pleasant. They understood the consequences of war.

In response to "the declaration of war made against this confederacy," Jefferson Davis made a speech on April 29, 1861, in which he made the South's position clear.[2] "We protest solemnly in the face of mankind that we desire peace at any sacrifice save that of honor and independence." All the Confederacy wanted, he said, was "to be let alone."[3]

President Lincoln would not allow the Union to be divided. Newspaper headlines in the North screamed for the Union Army to invade the South and bring the eleven seceded states back into the Union. Volunteers rushed to join the Union Army. Lincoln ordered a blockade on all Southern ports to prevent foreign ships from bringing in arms and ammunition.

Davis responded by inviting Southern shipowners to prey on Northern merchant ships and seize their cargo. Confederate raiders roamed the oceans

**"Dixie"**

This unofficial anthem of the Confederacy was never made official because many people thought it lacked dignity. Yet it was immensely popular and is still connected with the South today. The song was written for a New York minstrel show in 1859 and quickly became a hit. After the song was played at Jefferson Davis's Montgomery, Alabama, inauguration in 1861, it became the theme song of the South.

Union troops sometimes played and sang their own version of "Dixie." During the Battle of Fredericksburg, Union and Confederate troops were on opposite sides of the Rappahannock River. The Union Army's band performed songs for its troops, and when they played "Dixie," both sides cheered.

President Lincoln liked the song, too. After the war ended, he requested that "Dixie" be played at the White House as a symbol that it was a song for the entire nation.

in search of federal vessels laden with merchandise. Whenever they found such a vessel, they destroyed it and its cargo. Lincoln said these raiders were nothing more than pirates, and if caught, they would be hanged.

Meanwhile, the armies had to be trained. Union troops headed to Washington for training. Some of them marched through Maryland, and a riot broke out in Baltimore. Maryland was a border slave state, with many of its citizens loyal to the South. Angry to see Union soldiers in their town, they threw stones, bricks, and anything else they could find at them. A few soldiers reacted by firing their rifles at the crowd. People died—more civilians than soldiers—and many others were wounded.

Davis called a meeting to discuss the Baltimore situation. He hoped Maryland would join the Confederacy. He told his Cabinet they should adopt a policy to convince the border states to secede from the Union. Unfortunately for the South, Lincoln took steps so that would not happen. He sent Union troops to occupy Baltimore until the war was over.

## Organizing a New Government

Davis and his Cabinet spent long hours setting up the Confederate government. On May 20, 1861, the new Congress voted to make Richmond, Virginia, the Confederate capital. If the North invaded the South, it would be through Virginia, and everyone felt the government should be close to the action. Besides, Richmond was one of the South's few manufacturing and transportation centers, crucial to waging a successful war.

Davis arrived in Richmond on May 29. The next week, a train carrying Varina, Maggie, little Jeff, and baby Joseph pulled into Richmond. Besides suitcases and household goods, they brought Davis's horse and a "military saddle with a compass set into the pommel."[4] Rumors flew that Davis was planning to lead the troops into battle himself.

As much as Davis would have liked to lead the troops, he did not. He had a new country to run. However, he often visited recruits in the training camps in and around Richmond. Whenever he rode his horse through camp, soldiers waved their hats and cheered.

Davis called on his West Point friends, including General Robert E. Lee, to help plan Confederate war strategy. General Beauregard and his army were sent to northern Virginia to protect Virginia's railroads. The Manassas Gap Railroad connected Manassas with the Shenandoah Valley. General Joseph E. Johnston's troops would defend the Shenandoah Valley. Davis and Lee reasoned that these were the two avenues through which the Union Army would invade the South.

Many people urged Davis to launch an attack on Washington. He resisted. He feared that if he did, England and France, which Davis hoped would be sympathetic to the South, might change their minds and support the North. Davis needed them as allies. He was counting on England, France, and other countries to recognize the Confederacy as a separate nation.

In the North, newspaper editors and politicians were calling for action. Horace Greeley, editor of the New York *Tribune*, began the war cry, "Forward to Richmond."[5] Public outcry was so insistent that President Lincoln told General Irvin McDowell, commander of the Army of the Potomac, to invade the South. The general obeyed Lincoln's orders.

## The First Major Battle

On July 16, McDowell and his troops marched out of Washington. Two days later, they came to a winding little river called Bull Run. On the other side of the river, General Beauregard had positioned his troops at Manassas Junction. The first important battle of the Civil War took place there during the next few days. Historians call it the Battle of Bull Run or the First Battle of Manassas.

Davis had no intention of sitting in Richmond with the fighting going on only thirty miles away. As soon as he could get away, he headed for Manassas Junction. When the train arrived, the conductor said it was too dangerous to go any farther. Clouds of dust rose in the distance and passengers could hear the boom of cannons. Davis wanted to be on the battlefield, so he talked the conductor into detaching the locomotive and taking him as far as army headquarters.

At headquarters, Davis was given a horse and shown the route to the battle. As he approached the battlefield, the sound of artillery thundered through

*Confederate troops are shown here on their way to the battlefield near Manassas Junction. Confederate women serve refreshments to the troops at a station on the Manassas Gap Railroad.*

the air. He did not know if the Confederates had won or lost until he met some of Beauregard's staff. The enemy was in retreat, they told him, but still close enough to be a danger. They gave him an escort the rest of the way to the battlefield.

The retreat of the Union troops turned into a rout. The poorly trained Northern soldiers had panicked and were running back to Washington. But the road was jammed with horses and carriages, wagons

and sightseers. Hundreds of people had come out to watch the battle just two miles away.

Now everyone was in a panic to get back to Washington. The road was one big traffic jam, with terrified civilians, disorganized army troops, horses and carriages, and Union wagon trains and ambulances.

The First Battle of Manassas ended the illusion that war between the North and the South would be a short and glorious fight to prove whether the states would have one government or two. Both sides were shocked by the casualty figures—for the Union: 2,896 soldiers killed, wounded, or missing; and for the Confederates: 1,982.[6] Each side realized that before there could be another campaign, the armies would have to be properly trained and supplied.

Southerners celebrated the victory throughout the Confederacy. They believed the South would easily win the war. Davis was more realistic. He hoped Manassas was the beginning of the end of the war, but he foresaw problems.

The western part of Virginia had separated from Virginia and formed its own state—West Virginia— which was working toward becoming part of the Union. The citizens of West Virginia were pro-Union, and when Union General George B. McClellan took his army there, he met little resistance. Davis did not have enough troops to prevent the action.

Nor did he have enough troops and resources to protect the western part of the Confederacy. The Mississippi River ran down the middle of the Confederate nation—Arkansas, Texas, the Indian Territory, and part of Louisiana lay west of the river. Davis knew that if the Union ever got control of the river, the Confederacy would be cut in two.

## 1862

For Davis, 1862 was a year of high hopes and bitter disappointments. Since England needed Southern-grown cotton for its mills, Davis still hoped that the country would break the blockade and ally itself with the South. The blockade was beginning to impede the South's ability to get supplies. He also hoped Southern victories would win independence from the North.

As the war expanded to the West, the South suffered some bitter defeats. In February, the Union Army, led by General Ulysses S. Grant, captured Fort Henry on the Tennessee River and Fort Donelson on the Cumberland River. This led to Union occupation of Nashville and threatened the heartland of the South.

Confederate General Albert Sidney Johnston took his troops to Corinth, Mississippi, to reorganize. General Grant led the Union Army to Pittsburgh Landing, twenty miles away. On April 6, the two sides met in the devastating Battle of

Shiloh. The Union lost thirteen thousand troops; the Confederates lost ten thousand.[7]

At the end of the first day, the Confederates captured Shiloh Church, a key position. But Grant refused to give up and received reinforcements during the night. The next day he counterattacked. During the furious fighting, Johnston was hit by a bullet. He bled to death on the battlefield. The Confederates fought bravely, but their reinforcements did not arrive, and they had to retreat.

A few weeks after Shiloh, the South also lost one of its most vital cities. New Orleans, Louisiana, was the largest city in the Confederacy and its most important port. Located where the Mississippi River empties into the Gulf of Mexico, New Orleans had become the South's richest city through its thriving trade.

On April 25, 1862, David Farragut and his squadron of Northern warships captured the city. The loss of New Orleans was a disaster for the Confederacy. This left Vicksburg, Mississippi, as the only fortified Southern city on the Mississippi River. Davis feared that soon the entire waterway, so vital to the South, would also be lost.

## War in the East

The ultimate goal of the Union Army was to capture the Confederate capital of Richmond. But Davis had found a brilliant war leader, Robert E. Lee, who thwarted every attempt the North made to take

Richmond. Lee believed the best way to defend against an enemy was to attack. In what came to be called the Seven Days' Campaign, Lee's army attacked General McClellan's Union troops. After a week of hard-fought battles, McClellan and his army retreated.

Lincoln then put General John Pope in charge of capturing Richmond. Lee's army fought Pope's on August 29 and 30 at Bull Run. The Second Battle of Bull Run (or Second Battle of Manassas) ended with another Confederate victory. Davis was jubilant when the Union Army was driven all the way back to Washington.

With new confidence in the South's ability to fight the North, Lee suggested that the Confederate Army invade Maryland. If they could win one battle there, he told Davis, Southern sympathizers in Maryland might rise up and secede. Davis very much wanted that to happen, because it might persuade Lincoln to negotiate peace. Then, European nations would recognize the Confederacy as an independent nation.

Davis approved Lee's plans, knowing that Lee's troops were badly outnumbered, did not have adequate arms, and were poorly outfitted. Davis believed Lee's daring strategy would give the South another victory.

While Davis anxiously waited in Richmond, Lee positioned his troops on a ridge overlooking Antietam

Creek in Sharpsburg, Maryland. On September 17, McClellan attacked Lee in a battle that raged all day, with neither side defeating the other. So many men died on both sides that it became the bloodiest single day of the entire Civil War.

Although the battle ended in a draw, Lincoln regarded it as a victory for the Union because the Confederate invasion of Maryland had failed. Antietam gave Lincoln the opportunity he had been looking for to issue his preliminary Emancipation Proclamation. On September 22, 1862, Lincoln

*President Lincoln (third from left) is pictured here, reading the Emancipation Proclamation to his Cabinet on September 22, 1862.*

declared that as of January 1, 1863, all slaves within any state that was in rebellion against the United States "shall be then, thenceforward, and forever, free."[8]

Davis was furious. He realized that Lincoln's Emancipation Proclamation could make the worst Southern nightmare come true. If slaves were freed and armed, they might turn on their former owners. As it turned out, there were no major slave revolts in the South during the war, despite Lincoln's proclamation. Many slaves were afraid to rebel and remained loyal to their masters. Others took a wait-and-see attitude.

Nevertheless, the Emancipation Proclamation kindled within Southerners a fiery determination

**Emancipation Proclamation**
Emancipation means freedom. On September 22, 1862, President Lincoln issued a warning that he would free all slaves in states rebelling against the Union on January 1, 1863. The order did not include slaves in the border states still loyal to the Union. Not only were there constitutional problems that limited Lincoln's action in those states, but he also feared that if he banned slavery in those states, they would secede and join the Confederacy. Slaves in the border states gained their freedom in 1865 when the Thirteenth Amendment was added to the Constitution. This amendment outlawed slavery throughout the nation.

*After the Emancipation Proclamation, some former slaves fled northward from the war. Others waited to see what would happen. Here, a black family, fleeing slavery, crosses the Rappahannock River in Virginia to Northern lines.*

"to resist to the death a power that had no respect for property rights or constitutional guarantees."[9] Though the South was feeling the heavy burden of war losses, decreasing supplies, and shortages of civilian goods, the Confederate flag still flew defiantly. Jefferson Davis still believed the South could win its independence.

# 8

# HARD TIMES IN THE SOUTH

Southern fortunes plummeted in 1863, and critics blamed Davis for everything that went wrong. Newspaper editors attacked his military policy. They said the war in the West was going badly because Davis had neglected that part of the Confederacy. The real problem was that the Confederate Army did not have enough soldiers to cover battles in both the East and the West. When congressmen and some members of Davis's own Cabinet criticized his administration, he clammed up and told them as little as possible. In return, they called him a dictator, saying he did not consult with them enough. The criticism hurt Davis deeply.

Varina knew that her husband should have been communicating with these men, even flattering them, as politicians often do. But Davis did not have that kind of personality. While he could inspire soldiers on the battlefield, he was unable to do the same with Confederate congressmen.

At least the common people still believed in him. Davis was convinced that the South could outlast the North, and people continued to make enormous sacrifices.

The Union blockade of Southern ports was having a significant effect on the South, however. Food and supplies were being choked off, and there were not enough guns to go around. Uniforms were ragged, and many men even had to march and fight without shoes. Whenever they won a battle, Confederate soldiers removed the shoes from the Union dead and took their weapons.

Food was in short supply, too. Southern railroad transportation was poor, making it difficult for food and supplies to reach the soldiers. Also, so many small farmers had joined the army, there were few left to work the fields. Women tried to keep up the farms, but often crops failed or did not get planted at all. Cows, pigs, and chickens, as well as horses, were confiscated for the army, which left civilians without meat, milk, and transportation.

Food prices rose daily, and women, the sole providers when their men went off to war, could no

*As times became hard, Confederate troops were seldom able to wear the regulation uniform, as shown by these captured Confederate soldiers.*

longer afford to feed their families. In the spring of 1863, bread riots broke out in a number of Southern cities. In Richmond on April 2, a mob of women marched down Main Street, shouting "Bread! Bread! Give us bread for our children . . ."[1] The women rushed into stores along the way and took whatever they could find: flour, cornmeal, slabs of meat, shoes, and even jewelry. Davis urged the crowd to go home. He said they must put up with the hardships caused by the Northern invaders, who were "the authors of all our sufferings."[2]

Davis knew he had to do something to help his hungry people. Lee had the answer. The South was being ravaged by Union invasions. Why not take the war to the North? he asked. The Confederate forces had recovered from the Battle of Antietam and had won a great victory at Chancellorsville (May 2–4). The Confederate fighting spirit had never been better. Lee proposed to lead his troops north in a raid on Pennsylvania farm country, which was filled with livestock and other food.

## Battles of Gettysburg and Vicksburg

On July 1, 1863, Confederate troops clashed with the Union Army in the small town of Gettysburg, Pennsylvania, and forced the Northern troops to retreat. But during the night, Union reinforcements arrived. On July 2, the two sides fought mightily and suffered large numbers of casualties. Confederate reinforcements failed to arrive for the battle on July 3. To make matters worse, Southern troops ran short of ammunition. When Confederate troops ran across an open field into withering enemy fire on July 3, they slumped to the ground by the thousands. Lee lost nearly one third of his army. He could do nothing but retreat. The Union troops were in no shape to pursue Lee's battered army.

During this time, Davis waited anxiously in Richmond for news from Pennsylvania, as well as from Mississippi, where the Battle of Vicksburg was raging at the same time. He paced the floor day and night, unable to eat or sleep, and he became ill. Lee's note, telling him of the defeat at Gettysburg, finally arrived. Lee blamed himself for the failure. He later offered to resign, but Davis had no intention of replacing his best general.

On the Mississippi front, Davis learned that Vicksburg had fallen to Union forces led by General Ulysses S. Grant on July 4. Seventy thousand Union troops had surrounded the city. Trapped inside were

This painting shows a view of the Gettysburg battlefield, where each side suffered more than twenty thousand casualties.

twenty-eight thousand Confederate soldiers in addition to the city's residents. After a forty-seven-day siege, starvation set in and Vicksburg surrendered.

With the entire Mississippi River under Union control, the Confederacy was split in two. Texas, Arkansas, Indian Territory, and western Louisiana were cut off from the rest of the seceded states. Newspapers furiously attacked Davis, and civilian confidence began to erode.

There were no more major battles in the East for the rest of the year, but in the West, a major battle

was brewing. Confederate troops had trapped the Union Army in Chattanooga, Tennessee, and hoped to starve the men into submission, just as the Union had done to the Confederates in Vicksburg. Lincoln destroyed their hopes when he sent powerful reinforcements to break the siege. On November 25, the badly outnumbered Confederates withdrew to Georgia.

By the end of 1863, the Confederacy was being crushed by staggering problems. The new nation was facing bankruptcy. The Northern blockade was strangling its economy. The transportation system had broken down. Much Confederate territory had been lost, and the people were hungry and tired of war. Yet even with the odds of the Confederacy winning its independence diminishing each day, Davis had faith that the South could still become a separate nation.[3]

## 1864–1865

Disaffection with Davis and the Confederate cause rose dramatically in 1864. The defeats suffered by the army demoralized the troops and disheartened the people at home. Southerners were tired of the hardships they had to endure. Yet Davis was determined to keep the cause alive.

The South's greatest need was manpower. As morale plummeted, increasing numbers of soldiers deserted the army. Davis demanded that soldiers who were absent without leave return to their units.

General Lee wrote Davis that every man eligible for military service should be enlisted. Davis was so desperate for troops that he considered, but rejected, the radical idea of using slaves as soldiers.

The Union Army had been filling its manpower needs with blacks (and European immigrants) since the Emancipation Proclamation. Many were former slaves who had fled north after the war began. These newly liberated slaves were called contrabands.

The problems that Davis faced in 1864 were so overwhelming that his extraordinary self-control

### Contrabands

Contrabands were former slaves who fled to Union lands in 1861 and 1862. They had escaped from slavery but were not yet free. Slaves' status as property made them a war prize of the North. Union soldiers set the slaves free and gave them jobs in their army camps. Contrabands built roads and fortifications and did all kinds of military chores. They cleaned latrines, dug earthworks (barricades), drove ambulances, and performed long hours of guard duty—all the things the white troops did not want to do.

As the war progressed, the number of contrabands increased, and Union troops were followed by long lines of fugitive slaves who looked to the Northern armies to provide for their general welfare. Many contrabands joined the Union Army when they were allowed to enlist in 1863.

what was called the Wilderness Campaign, Grant lost more men than Lee had in his entire force, but kept attacking.[6]

Davis often rode out to the battlefield. One of the generals wrote,

> [H]e was an inspiration to every soul who saw him. He did not once interfere, suggest or order anything, but he was there demonstrating his readiness, and I have often thought his purpose, to assume control should the desperate moment arrive.[7]

By the summer of 1864, many Northerners had grown tired of war. Grant was no closer to capturing Richmond than he had been when the war began. Sherman seemed to be stuck in Georgia. A growing number of Northerners were calling for peace, and Lincoln feared he would not be reelected if the war dragged on.[8]

Davis hoped the Confederate armies could hold off Grant and Sherman until after the November elections. The South's best chance for independence would come if Lincoln were defeated. If the North were not winning the war by November, Lincoln's Democratic opponent and former leader of the Union Army, George McClellan, would probably be elected. Antiwar Democrats were ready to make peace.

Unfortunately for the Confederacy, things did not work out the way Davis wished. Sherman overpowered the Confederate troops protecting

**Copperheads**

In the North, the Copperhead wing of the Democratic party was against the war. Copperheads wanted peace even if that meant recognizing the Confederacy as a separate nation. As a symbol, they wore Indian heads cut from copper pennies in their lapels.

Atlanta, Georgia, and set fire to the city. On November 15, he began his 285-mile march to the sea, burning and pillaging everything in his path. On December 22, he reached Savannah, Georgia, and gave the city to Lincoln as a Christmas gift. Then he headed for Richmond. Meanwhile, General Sheridan was devastating the Shenandoah Valley, destroying the primary food supply for Lee's army.

Because he knew the Confederates were fighting against impossible odds, Davis sent out feelers for one last chance at negotiated peace. Lincoln responded that he was willing to discuss "securing peace to the people of our one common country."[9]

Davis sent three commissioners to meet Lincoln, instructing them, "It will never do to ignore the fact that there are *two* countries instead of but *one common country*. . . . We can't be too particular on that point."[10] The commissioners met with Lincoln on February 3, 1865. After three hours, the conference broke up. Lincoln would consider no terms except

for the South to lay down its arms and rejoin the Union. That, of course, was unacceptable to Davis. His felt his only recourse was "to fight to the finish."[11]

By the end of March, Grant had nearly surrounded Richmond and was about to cut the last escape route from the capital. Davis sent his family, which now included a baby daughter named Varina Anne (Winnie), to safety in Charlotte, North Carolina. Everyone knew Richmond would soon have to be abandoned.

## Richmond Falls

On Sunday, April 2, 1865, Davis received a message from Lee. It brought bad news. Grant had broken through the Confederate lines, and the Union troops were on their way to Richmond.

Davis called the Cabinet to his office. He told them to pack up as many government records as they could. They would move the capital south to Danville, Virginia, where Lee would march to meet them.

News spread quickly through Richmond that the government was evacuating. People were frightened, and anyone who could get any kind of transportation left town. Explosions rocked the city as Confederate troops destroyed anything of value that the Union might use. By the time Davis and his Cabinet left that night, the city was in flames.

*This is a view of a Union supply train as it moves through Petersburg, Virginia.*

As soon as Davis arrived in Danville, he set up his offices and asked for news from Lee. There was none, but Davis was expecting him hourly.[12]

The next day, Davis paced back and forth. Where was Lee? Finally he could stand it no longer and sent a messenger to find Lee. In the meantime, Lee had sent a young lieutenant to Davis with bad news: The Confederate Army had lost a third of its men and was surrounded by the enemy.

Davis, badly shaken, could not bring himself to believe that Lee would surrender. He was a brilliant

*This photograph shows the city of Richmond in ruins at the end of the Civil War.*

general, and Davis believed he would somehow find a way out.

On April 9, the messenger Davis had dispatched to find Lee came back with news no one wanted to hear. Lee had been forced to surrender to Grant in the village of Appomattox Court House, Virginia. The Army of Northern Virginia had given up. Davis was stunned, and those around him watched the Confederate president "silently weep bitter tears."[13]

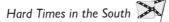

Before Davis could plan his next move, scouts burst into his office and announced that an enemy cavalry force was on its way to Danville.

Davis ordered an immediate withdrawal to Greensboro, North Carolina. General Johnston was there with the remaining Confederate Army in the East. They had not lost the war yet! The next day in Greensboro, Davis and his Cabinet met with Generals Johnston and Beauregard. Davis tried to persuade them to continue the war. But Johnston said everyone was tired of war and would no longer fight. Beauregard said any further resistance was

*General Robert E. Lee is pictured here, signing the Confederate surrender at Appomattox Court House, Virginia.*

hopeless. Everyone but Davis and one Cabinet member agreed.

That evening, Davis finally received a letter from Lee, describing the surrender. Davis cried as the reality finally hit him that the war might indeed be lost. Still, he would not admit defeat. He wrote Varina a note:

> I will come to you if I can—Everything is dark. You should prepare for the worst by dividing your baggage so as to move in wagons. If you can go to Abbeville it seems best as I am now advised . . . I have lingered on the road and labored to little purpose. My love to the children. . . . God bless, guide, and preserve you . . .[14]

*This picture illustrates Davis's "Government by the Roadside" at the end of the war. For a while, Jefferson Davis still tried to carry on the Confederate government as he fled from Union troops.*

## On the Run

Davis, his Cabinet, and a military escort made their way south, trying to avoid Union cavalry patrols. In Charlotte, North Carolina, Davis learned that President Lincoln had been assassinated in Washington on April 14, 1865. This was shocking news. Davis was even more horrified to learn that the new president, Andrew Johnson, had accused Davis of being part of the plot to murder Lincoln. Johnson declared Davis an outlaw and offered one hundred thousand dollars as a reward for his capture.

On the run now, the Davis caravan moved across North and South Carolina into Georgia. Realizing the cause was lost, Davis's Cabinet left him one by one to go back to their families or to save themselves from Union capture.

Davis finally caught up with his wife in Georgia. She was traveling in a wagon train with the children and a few friends, heading for safety in Florida. On the evening of May 9, 1865, they set up camp beside a creek just outside Irwinville. No one in the Davis camp knew that when Varina had passed through the previous town, someone had reported it to the Union Army.

Early the next morning, a Union trooper surprised Davis as he stepped outside the tent, and ordered him to halt. Davis was forced to surrender or be shot.

*This is an artist's depiction of the capture of Jefferson Davis in 1865.*

Davis, his family, and some other prisoners were loaded onto a boat that steamed up the East Coast. When the ship anchored near Fort Monroe in southern Virginia, Davis realized he was about to be imprisoned.

On May 22, 1865, Davis was transferred to a tugboat. Varina and the children walked down the gangway with him. At the bottom, he kissed his wife and children good-bye. He did not know when, or even if, he would ever see his family again. But he showed no emotion and whispered in Varina's ear, telling her not to show weakness by crying.[15]

# 9

# AFTER THE FALL OF THE CONFEDERACY

Davis spent nearly two years in Fort Monroe. At first he was placed in a small, damp cell with his ankles in chains, like a common criminal. His protests did no good. However, when word got out that the ex-president was chained up, there was such an outcry in all parts of the country that the leg irons were removed.

This was not Davis's only humiliating experience in prison. He received notes from former slaves saying how happy they were that he was in prison and that they had their freedom. Some people wrote letters saying he should be hanged for treason. The worst humiliation was the lie that spread through Northern newspapers saying Davis had tried to

escape capture at Irwinville by disguising himself as a woman.

Davis grew more depressed every day.[1] He could not eat, and the light that was kept burning in his cell all night kept him awake. By mid-summer, he was so weak that he had trouble walking. His doctor finally talked prison officials into moving him to a room on the second floor with fresher air. Davis's health began to improve. In August, he was finally given permission to correspond with his wife, which greatly cheered him.

Maggie, Willie, and Jeff, Jr., and had been sent to Canada at the end of the war to live with Varina's mother, who had joined the many Confederate refugees fleeing to Canada during and after the war. Varina had been detained in Savannah, Georgia, by Union authorities, and she kept baby Winnie with her.

Varina was not allowed to visit her husband for a year. When she finally saw him in May 1866, she was horrified by his "shrunken form and glassy eyes . . . his cheek bones stood out like those of a skeleton."[2] Though he was only fifty-seven years old, he looked like a feeble old man.

For the next three months, Varina made regular visits. Then she began a campaign to have her husband released from prison. She wrote to influential Northerners, including congressmen and the New York journalist, Horace Greeley. Ironically, Greeley

This is an illustration of Jefferson Davis (seated) in his prison cell at Fort Monroe.

was a leader of the antislavery movement. He wrote editorials in favor of either a speedy trial (Davis was being charged with treason), or releasing the ex-Confederate president on bail.

At the end of July, Varina Davis went to Washington and met with President Johnson to plead that her husband be set free. By this time, Northern opinion had changed. Davis's doctor at Fort Monroe, John J. Craven, had published a book, *The Prison Life of Jefferson Davis*, which became a best-seller. People all over the country, including abolitionists, demanded Davis's release. Even

President Johnson was sympathetic to Davis's plight. He suggested that Davis ask for a pardon in writing.

When Varina Davis reported this to her husband, he said he would never ask for a pardon. That would be a confession of guilt, and he still believed the Confederate cause was just. He wanted a trial in open court so he could prove the South had the right to secede. Davis was finally freed on May 11, 1867, after Greeley and a group of Northerners paid one hundred thousand dollars in bail, guaranteeing that Davis would show up for trial. A trial was never held, however, because the government never put together a case.

## A Man Without a Country

Upon his release from prison, Davis received many letters of congratulations and good wishes. Robert E. Lee wrote:

> Your release has lifted a load from my heart which I have not words to tell, and my daily prayer to the Great Ruler of the World is that he may shield you from all future harm, guard you from all evil and give you that peace which the world cannot take away.[3]

After his prison ordeal, Davis was extremely thin, with sunken cheeks and hollow eyes.[4] His beard and hair had turned completely gray.

Davis went to Montreal, Canada, for a joyful reunion with his children. Maggie, Jeff, Jr., and Willie were happy to have their loving father back, and Davis was thrilled to see them again.

*These are the children of Jefferson and Varina Davis, from left—young Jeff, Maggie, Varina Anne (Winnie), and Willie—as they were photographed in Montreal around 1867.*

The Davises received many social invitations in Montreal, but Davis preferred to stay out of the public eye. Varina sometimes found him "lost deep in distracted thought and occasional depression."[5] He worried because he had no home and no way to support his wife and children. Jobs were scarce in Canada for the many Confederate refugees. Davis hated living off the charity of friends, who anonymously paid the rent on the house where he and his family lived.

In 1868, the Davises went back to Mississippi and visited Brierfield. They were stunned to see their plantation overgrown with weeds and brambles, and to learn that their house had been used as a home for freed slaves. They visited friends and relatives, seeing only misery and poverty. Davis decided he was not ready to return to the South.

Davis's health was still fragile, so his doctor advised a year in Europe. In the summer of 1868, Davis moved his family to Great Britain. He

**The Lost Cause**
After they lost the Civil War, Southerners came to idealize the "Old South," which they believed was ruined by Northern aggressors. They remembered their attempt at independence from the North as the Lost Cause. After Jefferson Davis was imprisoned, he became a Southern hero and the beloved symbol of the Lost Cause.

enjoyed the country, where he was entertained by English gentry—lords and ladies, dukes and earls. He also visited Confederate friends who had moved to Great Britain. Davis looked for a job, but businesses wanted to hire only energetic young men, not someone who was sixty-one years old (and looked much older!). His hair was totally white and his face, though still handsome, was deeply lined. However, he still stood as tall and straight as he had as a military officer.

## Davis Finds a Job

Finally, Davis was offered the presidency of the Carolina Life Insurance Company in Memphis, Tennessee. During the late 1860s and 1870s, insurance companies and railroads often hired high-ranking former Confederates to be executives for their name recognition. In October 1869, Davis sailed back to America, leaving Varina and the children in London until he got settled.

Davis increased business for Carolina Life. Part of his job was to travel around the South to stimulate new accounts. What he saw on his travels made him very sad. The Civil War had completely changed the Southern way of life. Industry and agriculture were in ruins. Plantation houses were in disrepair, their verandas and fences falling down. The former slaves, although free, were as poor as everyone else, with neither land nor jobs. Many freed slaves were treated like serfs, still working the plantations for white owners.

In August 1870, Davis sailed to Liverpool to get his family. He was happy to see how well his children were turning out. Maggie was fifteen and a most delightful young lady. Thirteen-year-old Jeff and nine-year-old Willie were sons any man would be proud of. Winnie was as lovable as ever at six years old.

The Davises returned to America and settled in Memphis. Then a series of disasters happened. In October 1872, Willie died of diphtheria, a disease that today is prevented by immunization. Davis was grief-stricken, though in his stoic way he kept his misery to himself. He had now lost three of his four sons, and four years later his remaining son, Jeff, Jr., would die of yellow fever, a disease carried by mosquitoes. Then in 1873, a financial panic gripped the United States, and Carolina Life Insurance went out of business. At age sixty-five, Davis needed to find another job to support his family.

He thought about going back to Brierfield, but he did not have the energy to restore his ruined plantation. Mississippians asked him to run for a Senate seat, but he could not do that without being pardoned. Still, he would never ask for a pardon because that would mean confessing guilt for his part in the Civil War. He also refused to take an oath of allegiance to the United States, so he was no longer a citizen. Legally he could not represent his state.

## Davis Regains His Reputation

By the mid-1870s, Davis was enjoying increasing popularity. He was often invited to speak to veterans' groups and at agricultural fairs all over the South and in the West. Immaculately dressed, standing tall and thin before his audiences, he received standing ovations everywhere he spoke.

In 1877, Davis decided to write the book he had been thinking about ever since the war ended. He found a publisher who encouraged him, so he looked for a quiet place to write. A woman named Sarah Dorsey invited him to live in a cottage on her estate, called Beauvoir, on the Mississippi Gulf Coast. She was "a devout believer in the Confederate cause" and regarded Davis as "the noblest man she had ever met on earth."[6]

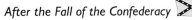

Beauvoir was a haven for Davis. After a few hours of writing, he could take a walk on the grounds, shaded by magnolias and other trees draped in gray moss. The Gulf of Mexico stretched out on one side of the house and an orange grove sprawled on the other side. Beyond that was a pine forest where he rode his horse. The murmur of the waves rolling onto the beach lulled him to sleep at night.

Varina did not move to Beauvoir until July 1878. She had spent many months in Europe where

*Jefferson Davis is shown here, seated on the porch of the Library Pavilion at Beauvoir.*

daughter Winnie was in school, and upon returning, she stayed with daughter Maggie in Memphis. When she saw how much Davis thrived in the serene environment of the Gulf Coast, she settled in the Beauvoir cottage and helped her husband with his book.

It took Davis three years to write *The Rise and Fall of the Confederate Government.* When Sarah Dorsey died on July 4, 1879, she left her estate to Davis. In her will she wrote, "I do not intend to share in the ingratitude of my country towards the man who is in my eyes the highest and noblest in existence."[7]

He was grateful for her gift. After years of strug-

gling to provide for his family, he had his own home at last. Beauvoir became a place for friends and admirers to gather. Davis was now considered a Southern hero, and invitations to give lectures poured in.

*Jefferson Davis, shown here with his granddaughter, spent the last years of his life enjoying his family and writing about his experiences as the president of the Confederacy.*

Everywhere he went, people gave him long standing ovations.

Davis celebrated his eightieth birthday at Beauvoir on June 3, 1888. During November of the following year, he made his last trip to his old plantation. In New Orleans, where he boarded the steamer *Laura Lee*, wintry weather drenched him with sleet and rain. Davis caught a severe chest cold. By the time he reached Brierfield, he had developed acute bronchitis. For four days he was ill in bed, until the plantation manager telegraphed Varina at Beauvoir.

Varina made arrangements to transport Davis to New Orleans. When the boat docked, an ambulance took him to the home of an old friend. Davis wanted to go back to Beauvoir, but doctors said he was too ill to travel. Varina tenderly nursed him for three weeks. He would not let her send word of his illness to their daughters. "Let our darlings be happy while they can," he said. "I may get well."[8]

On December 6, 1889, at the age of eighty-one, Jefferson Davis passed away.

# 10

# EPILOGUE

Jefferson Davis lay in state in New Orleans City Hall for three days and three nights, dressed in Confederate gray. Thousands of people filed by his copper-lined, black-draped casket. The lid of the casket was replaced by glass so that people could view his face. Ex-slaves from Brierfield came to pay their last respects. Mothers lifted up their children so they could see the former president of the old Confederacy. Veterans passed by, mourning their fallen leader. Fellow Southerners came to say farewell to the man who had dedicated his life to the South's struggle for its rights.

The funeral of Jefferson Davis was the grandest the South had ever seen. At noon, all the church bells in New Orleans rang and cannons boomed at one-minute intervals. Huge crowds lined the streets to watch the procession to the cemetery. Six black horses pulled the funeral carriage containing Davis's casket. A silk Confederate flag from Beauvoir was draped over the coffin, and Davis's sword from the Battle of Buena Vista was placed on top. Seven bands marched behind the carriage along with thousands of Confederate veterans, thirty aged Mexican War veterans, and fifteen Union veterans living in Louisiana.

After burying her husband, Varina went back to Beauvoir. In the Library Pavilion where Davis wrote *The Rise and Fall of the Confederate Government*, she came across the first few chapters of the autobiography he had begun. Varina decided the world should know what kind of man her husband was. She wrote a two-volume book, *Jefferson Davis: A Memoir by His Wife*, incorporating parts of his autobiography into more than sixteen hundred pages.

Because Varina's *Memoir* was published in New York, she made several trips there to make corrections before the book was printed. She liked the excitement of the city, and when the New York *World* offered her $1500 a year for a weekly article, she moved north.

Winnie also went to New York and worked for the *World*. Winnie had come to be called the "Daughter of the Confederacy" because she was born during the Civil War. She accompanied Davis on his speaking tours of the South during the last years of his life and often represented her father at Confederate gatherings. Her every move was watched by millions of Southerners. She dreaded what people would say when they learned that she planned to marry Alfred Wilkinson, a man from New York.

Many were horrified when they heard the news. Before his death, Davis had ignored their comments because he felt that marrying Wilkinson would be good for Winnie.[1] But she could not ignore the disapproval many Southerners expressed. She felt guilty that she might be causing distress to her father when she wanted to bring him only happiness.[2] Davis died thinking Winnie was going to marry Wilkinson. However, when Winnie's health declined and she went to Europe to recover, the couple drifted apart and never married. Winnie died in 1898 at the age of thirty-four.

Varina lived in New York for the rest of her life. She kept her husband's memory alive by signing her letters Varina Jefferson Davis, and she defended his reputation whenever anyone criticized him. She also arranged to turn Beauvoir into a shrine to Jefferson Davis. The house and Library Pavilion became a museum.

In 1893, Varina decided on the permanent burial place of Jefferson Davis. Mississippi felt he should

**Davis Regains His Citizenship**

It took more than a hundred years for Jefferson Davis to become a citizen of the United States again. In 1979, during the presidency of Jimmy Carter, Oregon Senator Mark Hatfield ushered a bill through Congress restoring the civil rights that Davis lost in 1865. (President Andrew Johnson had denied the rights of citizenship to Robert E. Lee, Jefferson Davis, and others who had supported the Southern cause.) Although Davis refused to swear allegiance to the United States for the rest of his life, he urged Southerners to support the new union of states after the war.

be laid to rest in the state where he had spent most of his life. Kentucky begged her to bury Davis in the state where he had been born. But it was Virginia's appeal that pleased her the most:

> Virginia holding in her loving embrace the sacred graves of five Presidents of the United States opens wide her arms and asks that she may be permitted to guard the last resting place of the President of the Confederate States. Here let us erect a monument that will stand in lofty and lasting attention to tell our children's children of our love for the memory of Jefferson Davis![3]

In late May, Davis's body was removed from his temporary tomb in Louisiana and taken by train to Richmond. At stations along the way, crowds turned out to pay their respects, showering the tracks with flowers.

*This is the Jefferson Davis Memorial in Richmond, where the Confederate president was buried after a moving appeal from the state of Virginia.*

Jefferson Davis was buried in Hollywood Cemetery in Richmond, Virginia, not far from the final resting places of former Presidents James Monroe and John Tyler. Eventually, Davis's entire family was buried beside him: Varina (who died in 1906), his six children, his son-in-law, and several grandchildren. Though it had taken him many years during his life, Jefferson Davis finally had won back his reputation. After his death, his legacy has lived on as one of the most respected leaders in American history.

# CHRONOLOGY

1808—Born on June 3.

1824—Father dies on July 4.

1824
–1828—Attends the United States Military Academy at West Point.

1828—Begins military career.

1835—Marries Sarah Knox Taylor on June 17; Resigns from army on June 30; Wife Sarah dies on September 18.

1845—Marries Varina Howell on February 26; Elected to the United States House of Representatives.

1846—Resigns from Congress to command the Mississippi Rifles in the war with Mexico.

1847—Becomes a hero in the Battle of Buena Vista; Mississippi legislature chooses him to fill a vacant United States Senate seat.

1848—Elected to six-year Senate term.

1851—Resigns from Senate to run for governor of Mississippi; Narrowly loses.

1852—Son Samuel Emory is born on July 30.

1853—Becomes secretary of war.

1854—Son Samuel Emory dies in June.

1855—Daughter Margaret is born on February 25.

1857—Son Jefferson, Jr., is born on January 16; Davis begins another term as United States senator.

1859—Son Joseph is born on April 18.

1860—South Carolina secedes from the United States on December 20.

1861—Six more states secede; Elected provisional president of the Confederate States of America on February 8; The South bombards Fort Sumter on April 12; The Civil War begins; Son William is born in December.

1862—Inaugurated as permanent president of the Confederacy on February 22; Lincoln issues the Emancipation Proclamation on September 22.

1863—The South loses Battles of Gettysburg and Vicksburg in July; Lincoln delivers Gettysburg Address in November.

1864—Son Joseph dies on April 30; Daughter Varina Anne (Winnie) is born on June 27.

1865—Davis and his Cabinet evacuate Richmond on April 2; General Robert E. Lee surrenders at Appomattox Court House, Virginia, on April 9; Davis is captured on May 10.

1865—Spends two years in prison.
–1867

1872—Son Willie dies October 16.

1877—Moves to Beauvoir in Mississippi to begin writing his book, *The Rise and Fall of the Confederate Government.*

1878—Son Jefferson, Jr., dies on October 10.

1889—Jefferson Davis dies on December 6.

# CHAPTER NOTES

### Chapter 1. Inauguration

1. Varina Davis, *Jefferson Davis: A Memoir* (Baltimore: The Nautical & Aviation Publishing Company of America, 1990), vol. 2, p. 180.

2. Hudson Strode, *Jefferson Davis: Confederate President* (New York: Harcourt, Brace and Company, 1959), p. 201.

3. Dunbar Rowland, *Jefferson Davis, Constitutionalist: His Letters, Papers and Speeches* (Jackson: Mississippi Department of Archives and History, 1923), vol. 5, p. 198.

4. Ibid., p. 200.

5. Ibid., p. 202.

### Chapter 2. Childhood

1. William C. Davis, *Jefferson Davis: The Man and His Hour* (Baton Rouge: Louisiana State University Press, 1991), pp. 10–11.

2. Ibid., p. 12.

3. Ibid., p. 17.

4. Hudson Strode, *Jefferson Davis: American Patriot* (New York: Harcourt, Brace and Company, 1955), p. 27.

5. Varina Davis, *Jefferson Davis: A Memoir* (Baltimore: The Nautical & Aviation Publishing Company of America, 1990), vol. 1, p. 29.

6. Strode, p. 24.

7. Varina Davis, p. 32.

8. Ibid., p. 33.

9. Ibid., p. 34.

10. Ibid., p. 54.

11. Ibid., p. 51.

12. William C. Davis, p. 38.

### Chapter 3. Frontier Army Life

1. Varina Davis, *Jefferson Davis: A Memoir* (Baltimore: The Nautical & Aviation Publishing Company of America, 1990), vol. 1, p. 67.

2. Ibid., p. 64.

3. Ibid., p. 80.

4. Hudson Strode, *Jefferson Davis: American Patriot* (New York: Harcourt, Brace and Company, 1955), p. 59.

5. William C. Davis, *Jefferson Davis: The Man and His Hour* (Baton Rouge: Louisiana State University Press, 1991), p. 72.

6. Ibid.

7. Ibid., p. 76.

## Chapter 4. Politics and Marriage

1. Varina Davis, *Jefferson Davis: A Memoir* (Baltimore: The Nautical & Aviation Publishing Company of America, 1990), vol. 1, p. 191.

2. William C. Davis, *Jefferson Davis: The Man and His Hour* (Baton Rouge: Louisiana State University Press, 1991), p. 98.

3. Ibid., p. 89.

4. James T. McIntosh, ed., *The Papers of Jefferson Davis* (Baton Rouge: Louisiana State University Press, 1974), vol. 2, p. 390.

5. William C. Davis, p. 122.

6. Hudson Strode, *Jefferson Davis: American Patriot* (New York: Harcourt, Brace and Company, 1955), p. 150.

7. Howard Zinn, *A People's History of the United States* (New York: Harper & Row, 1980), p. 147.

8. William C. Davis, p. 128.

9. Ibid., p. 157.

10. Perry Scott King, *Jefferson Davis* (New York: Chelsea House, 1990), p. 45.

11. William C. Davis, p. 182.

## Chapter 5. Spokesman for the South

1. Hudson Strode, *Jefferson Davis: American Patriot* (New York: Harcourt, Brace and Company, 1955), p. 241.

2. Dunbar Rowland, *Jefferson Davis, Constitutionalist: His Letters, Papers and Speeches* (Jackson: Mississippi Department of Archives and History, 1923), vol. 2, p. 17.

3. Strode, p. 268.

4. Hudson Strode, *Jefferson Davis: Private Letters (1823–1889)* (New York: Harcourt, Brace and World, Inc., 1966), p. 78.

5. Hudson Strode, *Jefferson Davis: Confederate President* (New York: Harcourt, Brace and Company, 1959), p. 69.

6. William C. Davis, *Jefferson Davis: The Man and His Hour* (Baton Rouge: Louisiana State University Press, 1991), p. 245.

7. James M. McPherson, *Battle Cry of Freedom: The Civil War Era* (New York: Oxford University Press, 1988), p. 151.

8. Strode, *American Patriot*, p. 301.

9. McPherson, p. 230.

10. Geoffrey C. Ward, *The Civil War: An Illustrated History* (New York: Alfred A. Knopf, 1990), p. 26.

## Chapter 6. Confederate President

1. Dunbar Rowland, *Jefferson Davis, Constitutionalist: His Letters, Papers and Speeches* (Jackson: Mississippi Department of Archives and History, 1923), vol. 5, p. 37.

2. Varina Davis, *Jefferson Davis: A Memoir* (Baltimore: The Nautical & Aviation Publishing Company of America, 1990), vol. 1, p. 697.

3. Rowland, p. 43.

4. Ibid., p. 42.

5. Davis, p. 699.

6. Rowland, p. 45.

7. Varina Davis, *Jefferson Davis: A Memoir* (Baltimore: The Nautical & Aviation Publishing Company of America, 1990), vol. 2, p. 19.

8. Rowland, p. 48.

9. Davis, vol. 2, p. 80.

## Chapter 7. Civil War

1. C. Vann Woodward, ed., *Mary Chesnut's Civil War* (New Haven: Yale University Press, 1981), p. 90.

2. William C. Davis, *Jefferson Davis: The Man and His Hour* (Baton Rouge: Louisiana State University Press, 1991), p. 329.

3. Dunbar Rowland, *Jefferson Davis, Constitutionalist: His Letters, Papers and Speeches* (Jackson: Mississippi Department of Archives and History, 1923), vol. 5, pp. 67–84.

4. Davis, p. 539.

5. Geoffrey C. Ward, *The Civil War: An Illustrated History* (New York: Alfred A. Knopf, Inc., 1990), p. 62.

6. Charles Plato, *The Civil War* (New York: Golden Press, 1960), p. 36.

7. Bruce Catton, *The Civil War* (Boston: Houghton Mifflin Company, 1960), p. 60.

8. Cass Canfield, *The Iron Will of Jefferson Davis* (New York: Harcourt Brace Jovanovich, 1978), p. 93.

9. Hudson Strode, *Jefferson Davis: Confederate President* (New York: Harcourt, Brace and Company, 1959), p. 314.

## Chapter 8. Hard Times in the South

1. Hudson Strode, *Jefferson Davis: Confederate President* (New York: Harcourt, Brace and Company, 1959), p. 381.

2. Ibid., p. 382.

3. Ibid., p. 513.

4. Varina Davis, *Jefferson Davis: A Memoir* (Baltimore: The Nautical & Aviation Publishing Company of America, 1990), vol. 2, p. 814.

5. Ibid., p. 497.

6. Cass Canfield, *The Iron Will of Jefferson Davis* (New York: Harcourt Brace Jovanovich, 1978), p. 106.

7. Strode, pp. 40–41.

8. Bruce Catton, *The Civil War* (Boston: Houghton Mifflin Company, 1960), p. 212.

9. William C. Davis, *Jefferson Davis: The Man and His Hour* (Baton Rouge: Louisiana State University Press, 1991), p. 590.

10. Ibid., p. 591.

11. Strode, p. 145.

12. Hudson Strode, *Jefferson Davis: Private Letters (1823–1889)* (New York: Harcourt, Brace and World, Inc., 1966), p. 151.

13. Burke Davis, *The Long Surrender* (New York: Vintage Books, 1989), p. 68.

14. Strode, *Private Letters*, p. 152.
15. Burke Davis, p. 175.

## Chapter 9. After the Fall of the Confederacy

1. Burke Davis, *The Long Surrender* (New York: Vintage Books, 1989), p. 205.
2. Ibid., p. 215.
3. Hudson Strode, *Jefferson Davis: Tragic Hero* (New York: Harcourt, Brace and World, Inc., 1964), p. 314.
4. William C. Davis, *Jefferson Davis: The Man and His Hour* (Baton Rouge: Louisiana State University Press, 1991), p. 658.
5. Ibid.
6. Hudson Strode, *Jefferson Davis: Private Letters (1823–1889)* (New York: Harcourt, Brace and World, Inc., 1966), p. 445.
7. Strode, *Tragic Hero*, p. 443.
8. Varina Davis, *Jefferson Davis: A Memoir* (Baltimore: The Nautical & Aviation Publishing Company of America, 1990), vol. 2, p. 930.

## Chapter 10. Epilogue

1. William C. Davis, *Jefferson Davis: The Man and His Hour* (Baton Rouge: Louisiana State University Press, 1991), p. 686.
2. Hudson Strode, *Jefferson Davis: Tragic Hero* (New York: Harcourt, Brace and World, Inc., 1964), p. 499.
3. Ibid., p. 529.

# GLOSSARY

**abolitionist**—A person who favored putting an end to slavery.

**annexation**—Incorporating territory into an existing country or state.

**armory**—A building for storing arms and military equipment.

**arsenal**—A place for storing, manufacturing, or repairing military weapons and ammunition.

**blockade**—Closing off a city, coast, or harbor with ships or military forces to control who goes in or out of it.

**Cabinet**—A group of advisors chosen by the head of a government to aid in administration.

**civil war**—A war between different groups or regions of one country.

**coexist**—To exist together without war or interference.

**compromise**—Settlement of differences in which each side gives up something it wants.

**Confederacy**—The eleven Southern states that seceded from the United States in 1860–1861.

**disunion**—Separation.

**earthwork**—A bank of earth piled up, usually used as a military fortification.

**expansionist**—A person who believes in increasing or adding to the territory of a country.

**extremist**—A person who goes to extremes, especially in politics.

**proclamation**—An official announcement.

**provisional**—Temporary.

**reconciliation**—Settlement of disagreements or differences.

**secede**—To formally withdraw from an organization.

**sovereign**—Self-governing; independent of the control of other governments.

**treason**—Betrayal of one's country such as by waging war against it.

**Union**—The twenty-three states that remained in the United States during the Civil War.

# FURTHER READING

Davis, William C. *A Concise History of the Civil War*. Eastern National Park and Monument Association, 1994.

Kent, Zachary. *The Civil War: "A House Divided."* Springfield, N.J.: Enslow Publishers, Inc., 1994.

Kerby, Mona. *Robert E. Lee: Southern Hero of the Civil War*. Springfield, N.J.: Enslow Publishers, Inc., 1997

King, Perry Scott. *Jefferson Davis*. New York: Chelsea House, 1990.

Robertson, James I., Jr. *Civil War!: America Becomes One Nation*. New York: Alfred A. Knopf, 1996.

## Internet Address

Parker, M. Donald. *Welcome to Beauvoir: Last Home of President Jefferson Davis*. April 21, 1997. <http://www.beauvoir.org/>.

Williams, Kenneth H. *The Papers of Jefferson Davis*. April 9, 1996. <http://www.jeffersondavis.rice.edu/>.

# INDEX